**Upcoming books to be released by Red Devine
"Learning to live life on a whole new level"**

<u>The Master Series</u>
How to Be a Kid Again
How to Win the war
Simple Truth -Spiritual Power
Spiritual Law- The Path

<u>Our Website:</u>
Reddevine.com
Email: <u>red@reddevine.com</u>
Authors Facebook
Twitter
You Tube

You can find us at:
Reddevine.com
red@reddevine.com
To receive our newsletter and join
"The Light Brigade" go to our website and register.
We will include you in our upcoming seminars and events
Nothing but Love

Written and Illustrated by

Red Devine

WESTBOW
PRESS®
A DIVISION OF THOMAS NELSON
& ZONDERVAN

All scriptures are from the KING JAMES VERSION (KJV): KING JAMES VERSION, public domain.

WestBow Press books may be ordered through booksellers or by contacting:

WestBow Press
A Division of Thomas Nelson & Zondervan
1663 Liberty Drive
Bloomington, IN 47403
www.westbowpress.com
1 (866) 928-1240

ISBN: 978-1-5127-9441-0 (sc)
ISBN: 978-1-5127-9442-7 (hc)
ISBN: 978-1-5127-9443-4 (e)

Library of Congress Control Number: 2017911108

Print information available on the last page.

WestBow Press rev. date: 10/18/2018

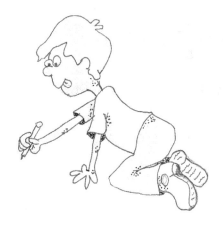

As you learn the secrets of childhood,
Grab a few Crayola crayons,
some markers and have fun coloring...
and don't worry about staying within the lines...

This book is dedicated to:

The Mother who brought me into this world, and the God who will someday take me out.

To my wife for her love and support, my soulmate and friend.

To my children and their spouses who are a constant reminder of what a miracle worker God is. And to my amazing grandchildren

My unending thankfulness and love to my brothers and sisters in Christ. Those I know and those I will soon meet.

What a great family to be part of.

Contents

Introduction

"Is There Any Hope?"

Searching for answers? Maybe you thought you'd found it, but then somehow, something changed.

If you're looking to get it back, then welcome, to a place where a cardboard box is fun, and you can see the amazing shapes in the clouds. It's time to learn the secrets of how to be a kid again.

The daily challenges of life can rob you of joy, steal your hope and kill your confidence in the future.

Monday becomes Tuesday, then there's Wednesday (hump day) and then Thursday, and here comes Friday. You go home, get in bed, wake up, it's Monday which becomes Tuesday, then there's Wednesday (hump day) and then it's...well it's life.

Years become months, months become weeks, days become hours, and then there are seconds to live. Life is short, and in that time, you either develop solutions or become boxed in by overwhelming problems. Looking for answers to eliminate the stress from the questions you cannot answer, seeking wisdom to overcome the challenges of life.

You either conform to this world or make the world conform to you, you either control your life or it will control you.

Is there hope? Somewhere along the way the battles you faced stole the most precious weapons you had as a child. You misplaced your toys, threw away your comics, and may have even lost all your marbles.

Life can cause you to grow up fast, barely having a childhood. To survive you had to get smart or the world would eat you alive.

You played the game with the hand you were dealt. The stakes were high, you went all in, putting joy, faith and peace in but when the cards were dealt you lost the hand. Because an inside straight always beats a pair of aces.

If you couldn't ante up, life was a confusing haze of failed relationships and unforeseen depression; living life in the shadows, searching for any light. Maybe you found your answers at the bottom of a bottle, or by using the latest designer drugs, looking good in the latest fashions, helping you hide from the truth. Looking for answers to the question, "Why?"

As kids we played, laughed, and watched the dawn when the sun raced to meet the sky. We knew the secret codes hidden in the clouds. When we fell, we picked up our bikes, dusted ourselves off and pedaled into the sunset, seeking new adventures, impervious to pain, believing we would live forever.

But everything is not lost: put aside the past to become a kid again. Hold fast to faith, renew your hope, abide in peace, encompassed in joy. When you let go and let God, your heart begins to understand the depth of love. Feeling the power of faith, recognizing peace, catching a case of overcoming truth.

Faith, love, and peace come from understanding the world as children see it. A world full of promise, knowing they can fly, even if others have their feet firmly fixed on the ground.

Was your childhood stolen? Can you remember life being wonderful? If you've failed finding peace of mind or desperately looking for hope, then it's time to play again.

Travel to exotic destinations, experience adventures and find that hidden treasure you've lost. When you click your heels together three times and say "Bora, Bora" you'll travel to magical far-away places using your un-filtered imagination and renewed child-like faith believing anything is possible.

It's time to learn the secrets, full of confidence about today with a renewed faith about tomorrow. Time to join this adventure of spirit and truth, where water balloon fights and slip and slides makes sense.

In this book you'll find Biblical stories that I've taken the liberty to expand from the original text. I felt Gods leading to tell the stories in a more detailed manner making the message come alive. I stayed true to the spirit of what was written and ask the reader to research the original text and find the Biblical background for each story. My hope is that this brings forward the feelings, emotions and power of what folks felt then and bring more color and understanding of the events of that time.

Jesus also did many other things. If they were all written down, I suppose the world could not contain the books that would be written.

John 21:25

It's my hope that what you are about to read gives you a new appreciation for the amazing life that Jesus led and the gifts He's giving to the world. Showing you of how to claim them for your own.

> *If you're depressed, you're living in the past;*
> *If you're anxious, you're living in the future;*
> *If you're at peace, you're living in the present.*

CHAPTER

1

Old Blue

Mistakes aren't a bad thing, they help you gain wisdom and a brand new approach to life. I learned that from an amazing coon hound "Old Blue" born and bred to be a hunter. His gift was that he never gave in, gave up, or gave out. He had a plan and executed it well.

It was his tenacity and ability to learn that made him who he was, the highest prize-winning raccoon hunting dog in the whole county.

When you eliminate the past, you find hope for the future. And learn how to live in a powerful, peaceful state no matter the situation. Remaining teachable is the pathway to creating a new life. *You need to yearn, to learn.*

Part of that was taking chances as a kid; it seemed the adventures would never end. There were a few bruised knees, one or two black eyes, and even a broken wrist from trying to walk a tightrope tied from the slide to the monkey bars put up to impress anyone looking. Each time something happened a lesson was learned, such as don't do things that will give you bruised knees, black eyes and broken wrists.

I wake up every morning now seeking new adventures, looking for fantastic and incredible journeys, yearning to learn. It's the desire that lights the fire. And Old Blue was lit up with it…

1964-One Eyed Jack

Most Families history in the Blue Ridge Mountains was as old as the hills they lived on. Wonderful friendly folk who, at the drop of a hat, would have you over for dinner, even if you just met. I've been in homes where you knew they had very little to give, but they were the first to share with you whatever little they had.

The traditions and family gatherings were legendary. Your neighbors were like family if anyone needed help, someone would show up and give of their time or expertise. After the chores were done it would be time to eat cornpone, grits, fried potatoes, and biscuits oozing with homemade butter and honey, and jam so full of fruit you had to dig it out with a spoon. We had fresh milk and spring water to drink, and fried chicken that would have made the Colonel turn in his apron, followed by Red Velvet Cake so moist and smooth it made velvet jealous. Once everybody's bellies were full, someone would pick up a guitar or a fiddle and the Bluegrass music would fly, from *Rocky Top* to the *Tennessee Waltz*.

I was raised in those hills and have wonderful fond memories of the Blue Ridge Mountains and the beautiful characters that lived there. Some of my greatest adventures came from there. Every morning there was chores to do, go to the well and get two pails of spring water. I'd go out where we stored our coal and clear the snow to get the biggest pieces for the furnace and gathering wood for the stove my grandma cooked on, it's crackling fire and welcome warmth in the winter made you feel cozy. And there was always a pot of coffee sitting on the side of the stove it's aroma filled the air. There was something about the taste of that food it had real flavor.

Drinking my first cup of coffee made me feel all *"growed"* up. It's was a simple and profound time. I built my first fort in those woods, fighting a battle with *"the Reds Coats"* securing freedom for America.

We'd drink pure fresh spring water gushing out of the rocks using a Mason jar tied there with an old piece of string. It hung on a branch for everyone to use. It was simple life-changing and more fun than watching a pig rolling in the mud.

We'd hunt and fish on the New River stopping by the general store where the local characters gathered, they sat around an old pot belly stove telling stories and making up lies.

On one particular day an older gentleman sitting by the potbelly stove called me over. *"Hey boy, would you like something good to chew?"* he asked. *"Yes sir,"* I said falling into his wily trap. He cut me a piece of this new stuff. I took it, thanking him, I should've known something was up as he winked and laughed while I chewed. I was waiting for this great new flavor to invade my mouth but instead it wasn't long before I had ten pounds of trouble in a five-pound bag. My mouth was on fire and there wasn't a fireman around for miles.

I ran to the bathroom like a Cheetah on speed I had to spit this stuff out, I could hear them laughing and slapping their knees in the background. My mouth was burning, my stomach churning, and I was looking for relief. It tasted like diesel oil wrapped in a mud wrapper sitting on a dusty shelf for ten or twelve years. I found a Mountain Dew and swallowed it whole. It barely put out the fire; back then the bottle read, *"It will tickle your Innards,"* and brother my innards needed tickling. I never touched anything with the name *"Chewing Tobacco"* on it again.

I'd hunt squirrels with my friends, walk down country roads, eat corn right off the stalk, feed the pigs, milk the cows. You could smell the honeysuckle bushes as you walked by, sweet and full of flavor. We would pull the flowers off and suck in the nectar. Wild blackberries and gooseberries would grow in the forest, sweet and tart, always careful of the thorns. You could live in that forest and never need to go to the *"Piggly-Wiggly"* again. It's a time I will never forget.

Down the road a piece was my best friend Talert. He joined me on many adventures in those woods and the back roads of our county. We were always looking for something new to do.

Once our uncles talked us into going *"Snipe"* hunting. We spent an hour or two in the forest holding a grocery bag and beating a tree yelling *"Here Snipe, over here, Snipe!"*

They sat there busting a gut. We never saw one, not then or ever. I really don't believe a three-legged purple bird with a green beak exists anyway. But we were always willing to try any high adventure.

Talert and I had done some crazy things that should have killed us, like building sleds to fly down a steep snowy hill. We didn't consider that at the bottom of that hill was a busy road, we narrowly missed Old Miss Simpsons 1952 Chevy Truck as she was coming back from church. I believe we all got closer to God that day.

We stole Mr. Wineberry's turnips, ate them right out of the ground, dirt and all. We chased a couple of bear cubs into the woods which, by the way, is not a good idea. They're cute when there small, but momma bear wasn't happy with us at all. It was the first time I climbed a tree without even touching it. So, when Talert asked me to go raccoon hunting, I had some trepidation, but it seemed safe enough since our uncles weren't involved. He explained that raccoons were small furry things that didn't seem like anything close to a bear, so I was all in.

We'd pushed the limits in the past, so I was a bit nervous. Just turning nine I had never been introduced to a raccoon. I was worried that Talert could be wrong, what if a raccoon was bigger than me? Talert had talked me into some crazy stuff, and if that raccoon was hungry who knew if it was possible to shinny up a tree carrying a gun.

When I got to Talert's house, it looked like a small army had prepared to go to war...we were going hunting with these fellas and it was evident they had been hunting for some *"Wild Turkey"* and found it. In fact, about four bottles of it. Most of them were as drunk as five ways to Sunday; to say that they felt no pain was a little like saying moonshine was a great healer. If you drank just a few swigs, believe me you no longer felt what was ailing you.

I made a quick decision to stay in the background since they had loaded up more than their guns.

Raccoon hunting is done at night and Mr. Johnson, Talert's dad, was a fine hunter and had some of the best hunting dogs any man could want. But none of his dogs were as valuable as Old Blue. He was a grand champion raccoon hunting dog. They said that if a raccoon was climbing on the Great Wall of China, he could smell it in the mountains and tree it in Mongolia before you could split a log.

As we got ready Talert's dad, began to open the dog cages. I tried to help by grabbing a few dogs, but they began to run as the dust was flying they howled like they were dancing on broken glass, *"OOwoo, OOwoo!"* They were chomping at the bit to get into woods, their bodies shaken with anticipation. Old Blue came out of his cage quiet and regal he looked at the other dogs with disgust. As he walked by every dog stayed back a piece from Old Blue. They knew who the boss was and not one of those blue tick hounds wanted anything to do him.

Trying to hold the dogs back I fell a couple of times to everyone's amusement, these fanatic dogs pulled their leashes, itching to get loose. I thought I would lose an arm. Mr. Smith looked at Mr. Johnson and said, *"You better let the boy loose from those dogs before they rearrange his looks."* I knew he was right, but I wasn't going to give up.

It was getting dark, and the old dirt road from Mr. Johnson's farm led into the woods behind the barn. Mr. Johnson leaned down and said, *"Look, boys, you need to be careful when you're shooting and for God's sake and the sake of your rear end, don't you lose Old Blue."* I was honored that Talert's dad trusted us with Old Blue. We made a spitting handshake promise to stay with that dog even if it killed us.

Suddenly, without a word, Mr. Johnson let the dogs go. The dogs were at a fever pitch, running out of their leashes like Houdini escaping chains. The dust began to fly, as we gathered ourselves together watching this small army deploy. We followed the dogs hot on their heels as they ran into the forest as if the devil himself was poking them along.

"OOwoo, OOwoo!" Old Blue leading the pack, he looked back at us wondering if we were coming. We looked at each other, and ran as fast as we could, trying to catch up with him. If he hadn't stopped for a moment picking up a scent, I'm sure we would have lost him.

Darkness fell, and the only light we had was our miner's lights. When I turned mine on it lit up Old Blue's face, he was determined, his face twisted and intense. He had this strange look as if a rare wind had blown over him picking up a scent of something he remembered or maybe wanted to forget. He headed into the south side of the forest.

On the North side of the road, the other dogs were chasing a raccoon that was scooting through the brush. We heard the dogs running and the leaves flying, Talert said *"They're getting close!"* Their howls changed from a deep bellow to a high-pitched scream.

Old Blue wasn't affected as he ran through that heavy forest; he was on task, something driving him. Mr. Johnson stayed back a piece making sure we were watching Old Blue. He knew something was wrong with his prize dog. *"Get going boys."* He said, *"Don't let Old Blue out of your sight!"*

Carrying our guns, we plunged into the forest. Dark and scary I wondered what I had gotten myself into. Then it began to rain. Great I thought what's next?

We started working our way through briars and twigs, our lights barely lit up Old Blue just ahead. I don't know if you've ever been in a Blue Ridge Mountain forest at night when it's raining; while your chasing a dog that had the uncanny ability of leading you through briars and bushes that skinned us up and ripped our clothes, it was brutal. And mud was easy to find as we tried to keep up.

He wasn't letting up, so we left our guns against an old oak tree. Not having the guns, it crossed my mind that there could be in trouble if we saw a raccoon. Because running up a tree would be our only defense. With my luck, any tree I'd climb would be filled with a family of hungry raccoons looking for a young kid to eat.

We finally caught up with Old Blue puffing and wheezing he seemed confused. He circled a tree looking befuddled. We could hear the echo of the other dogs' yelping and screaming. Talert said, *"Them boys have treed a coon!"* I heard someone say, *"Wow, boys, he's a big 'un!"*

We trudged through the brush. I felt like a blind man in a dark room looking for a black cat that wasn't there. I hoped that my Miner's light wouldn't run out, it was the only light I had. We entered a clearing and Old Blue sat there, quiet. We didn't know what he was chasing he looked ahead focused like a laser. Talert said it was like Old Blue was chasing a ghost. Suddenly he jumped up on an old log, and after checking it out, he dropped down and went back to following a trail through more blackberry vines. He backtracked trying to find the scent again, I'm sure the rain and darkness didn't help.

His frustration was evident as he stalked his prey. Then Old Blue sat down and made an awful noise. He was confused and lost, close to crying. The sound he made wasn't a high- pitched yelp but more like a slow, agonizing sob. He looked tired and worn out, so we sat down with him. I started petting him. The light from my Miner's light crossed his back and I could see scars from some earlier battle. He surely had his share of fights both won and lost.

This was my first raccoon hunt and it wasn't fun. We'd been cut by thorns from the blackberry bushes that had grabbed us like a tiger on the loose. It had gotten cold and nothing is as fun as being soaked, full of mud blinded by the frost of our heavy breathing. We sat there for a while making sure Old Blue was okay. He looked out into the darkness, he was searching for something.

We could hear the others coming back so Talert and I grabbed Old Blue, put a leash on him. He bellowed and fought a little, making that sad sound as if he had lost something. It wasn't until later that we learned what it was.

It was hard getting Old Blue out of the forest we could tell he had caught the scent of a lost memory or a found adversary. We had to get back to our guns, we grabbed them, slung them over our shoulders, and struggled back to the old dirt road. Talert's dad laughed a little, when he saw us we looked like we'd lost the war. The only thing you could see was our teeth and eyes. I stood there, mud dripping off my nose and made the intelligent decision, that raccoon hunting was not for me.

The other dogs came running up with their heads held high, proud that they had done their job. They cautiously circled Old Blue they seemed to sense his grief. He stood like a statue, focused on the forest. It looked like Old Blue had lost his way it was quiet as a funeral wake. I felt sorry for him. We headed back to the farm to put the other dogs away, Old Blue just shuffled into his kennel with a sound of disgust, his head turned away from of the forest. I gave him his food, but he didn't even look at it.

I tried to dry off, knocking the mountains of mud off my boots taking inventory of all the cuts and bruises I'd earned. It didn't take long to come to the brilliant conclusion that looking for a bear was more fun than chasing down a raccoon. I was never going to do this again!

A few weeks later, life taught me a critical lesson: never say, *"I'm never doing that again,"* Just as sure as the sun comes up and a rooster will crow, someone is going to make sure that you do.

Some time had passed since that night. Most of my cuts and bruises had healed. I went by Talert's hoping to start some new adventure. When I walked in, his dad asked if we wanted to go again.

"No" was going to be my definite answer, but Talert was waving and jumping around in the background. I touched my arm to feel the places where I'd been cut. They seemed to be healed up. Watching Talert, I had a weak moment, because somehow *"Yes"* came out of my mouth. I guess misery does love company, that's what friends are for.

Everything was the same the next night the dogs were yelping, pulling on their leashes, I was barely holding on. It wasn't long before we were back in the woods watching Old Blue, and just like last time, the pack went one way and Old Blue went the other. The only difference it wasn't dark and there was no rain. I felt at least this time I wasn't going to get wet.

Old Blue was heading back where we had been. But this time something was different. You could tell something was driving him. He started through the creek heading to the other side. Stopping for a moment then he headed further into the woods. All I could see was the creek in front of me.

Catching my friend's eye, I said, *"You got to be kidding me! I don't want to get wet again?"* I carefully crossed the stream stepping on stones hoping to stay dry. I was looking for Old Blue when my foot slipped, and I feel head first into the water. I came up spitting water. Talert laughed so hard he dropped his gun. I was mad at first, but soon I was laughing too.

As I got out of the stream I felt it was important to share. Talert tried to run but I caught him and gave him a big bear hug. It was the right thing to do. Now water was dripping off the both of us. For a minute we lost Blue and panicked, but he jumped up on an old log and we saw him, he was following the same trail as before.

Nothing was going to stop him this time his whole demeanor had solidified to the hunt. You could hear the muted sounds of the other dogs echoing through the trees in the distance. The same old song through the now dark forest. They had found something.

Old Blue raised his head not paying attention to their excited yelps. He went around that log making sure he was on the right path. He looked back and ventured ahead. Since it was dark we switched on our lights watching him go from tree to tree, considering a hole, stopping and going to the other side. Whatever he was tracking was going to be found. Whatever it was, thought on a whole different level it led us through an unbelievable obstacle course making sure we would pay the price for getting there. Old Blue hardly breathed or made a noise he had a definite plan.

He knew a trick when he saw it, and learned from his mistakes, I admired his determination and resolve. Going from this tree and that rock, looking in this hole and climbing that hill he was on task.

We were tired, cold and wet it was getting harder to get through the severe obstacles and unyielding brush we encountered. Whatever we were chasing made sure if we found him we'd have to unravel a very complex puzzle. We'd almost given up when we entered a meadow. Old Blue slowed down, intense and focused.

Right in front of us was a big old broken oak tree lit up by the rising full moon. We were exhausted and thankful to leave the forest behind. The big oak was scarred and torn I couldn't tell if it had been hit by lighting or survived a fire, but it had been through a few battles itself.

The wind traveled through its branches making a hollow low sound as if it was in pain. It was tall and haunted, at least if I were a ghost I'd hang out there. Getting closer, Old Blue began this little deep growl which made the hairs on my neck stand up. Sweat beaded up on my hands as my gun slipped a little. He raised his head looking up into the tree his growl wasn't an excited yelp but a confirming nod that we were there.

He'd followed a scent though the most difficult path any human or dog could take. It was incredible. His persistence kept him on course he never considered the past only what lied ahead. It was something the way he recognized every trick and knew every crooked path he encountered along the way. What he had learned through his battles kept us on course. He worked through the problems until he found the solution. He never gave up.

All of a sudden, I heard this most awful, grating, hissing sound, scarier than I'd ever heard before. It was coming from that old dead oak tree.

I held tight to my gun and backed up a little, looking around me not knowing what to expect. When I looked up I saw it, one big red eye looking down at us, cussing and spitting something awful. My heart skipped a beat I didn't know if I should shoot or run. I tried to move but was frozen in place afraid if I moved it would see me and attack. The air was charged with electricity as it began to rain. Lighting struck right in front of us, followed by a huge clap of thunder. It rolled past us like a wall of sound, obnoxious and loud. Dear God, I thought we've found the gates of Hell. I didn't know what one of the devil's imps sounded like, but I was sure we were finding out.

Suddenly, I thought to myself, snipe hunting seemed like a better thing to be doing right now.

There was a loud, strange noise to my left, there's nothing like the vision of a monster raccoon coming at you in a spooky forest at night to get you real close to Jesus. It sounded like a herd coming my way.

I wiped the sweat off my trembling hands aiming my gun towards whatever was coming. I was surrounded, branches were cracking, the noise getting louder, more intense, I closed my eyes hoping it would go away. It was creepy and scary, I could imagine a tribe of rabid raccoons after me led by this one-eyed monster.

I cocked back the hammer and sat behind the biggest tree I could find. If I was going to be the guest of honor at a raccoon's supper, a few of them were going with me.

Nervously pointing my gun into the darkness, even if I could get a shot off my gun was shaking so hard I wouldn't hit the side of a barn. the noise grew louder. Without warning a bright light blinded me. Just then the lighting struck again this time even closer. The thunder rolled through the forest like a ghost looking for someone to spook. The bushes parted I wiped the sweat from my face, started putting pressure on the trigger there he was standing in front of me. I took a breath and said a silent prayer. Was this the end of my life?

"*Whoa, I won't shoot if you don't shoot.*" As Mr. Johnson appeared. I dropped my gun feeling a little faint. "*What you boys got?*" he yelled. Talert and I looked at each other trying to figure out what to say. Then Talert said, "*We don't know, but he ain't happy.*" I was glad to see Mr. Johnson, at least now knowing that we had three of us to fight off any rabid invading raccoon army.

Old Blue sat there staring up at this one-eyed monster in the tree. Mr. Johnson looked up trying to find the source of that demon yell once he did he shook his head in disbelief. "*Well, I'll be a skinned rabbit looking for a fur coat to wear,*" he said "*That is the meanest, most ornery raccoon this forest has ever known, boys. That monster is One-Eyed Jack.*" I backed up making sure my gun was cocked and loaded.

Mr. Johnson reached down to pet Old Blue. As he did, his scars showed up with what little light we had. Talert looked up at his dad and in a reverent tone like he was praying in church, he said: "*Now I know why Old Blue has been acting so crazy.*" Mr. Johnson laid down his gun, and sat on a nearby stump, getting his pipe and proceeded to tell us a story when One-Eyed Jack had both his eyes and Old Blue had treed him.

It was Old Blue's first-time hunting and he had treed that raccoon in record time. It had shaken up One-Eyed Jack so much that he jumped from the tree with every intention of killing Old Blue. Mr. Johnson took a puff off his now lit pipe and said, "*It was an awful fight I had to hit One-Eyed Jack with a tree branch I found nearby to get him off Old Blue*" He pointed towards the scars on Old Blue's back telling us it was that battle that caused them. Old Blue had been hurt badly but he got his licks in and that was when Jack became One-Eyed Jack before escaping into the forest.

Speaking low and quiet he said *"Old Blue has been looking for this raccoon for years. "We just thought he'd died. But Old Blue never gave up; when he would hunt he would tree any raccoon that got in his way, but I knew he was looking for something else."* Just then Old Blue walked over to Mr. Johnson with confidence and pride. If he could have talked he would have said *"Y'all thought I was crazy."*

Almost on cue, One-Eyed Jack started yelling out his demon yell. Old Blue sat there, peaceful and serene, I reached down to make sure he was still breathing. I didn't take my eyes off that one red- eyed monster in that haunted old Oak tree. I thought I heard rustling leaves in the background. I turned in case something decided to show up.

Old Blue had a plan. During that first week as it rained he'd lost the scent and was frustrated, but I could tell that he didn't want to give up. I knew when we took him back to his kennel he was planning how to overcome that first week's failure. Whatever disappointment or pain he may have felt he put it aside. It was the battle and the pain that made Old Blue what he was, and he had the scars to prove it. Failure made him smarter and more determined to win. He shook off the past, focused on the present, and never gave up on the future, Old Blue had a plan.

That night we stood under that full moon, I felt God was smiling. Old Blue knew we'd win if we just didn't give up. There were times when we didn't understand, but we took a stand anyway.

While I sat there looking at the stars I'd peek at that big old haunted oak tree and the red-eyed devil that was screaming. I held tight to my gun making sure I was ready for his next move. We started to get up the clouds started moving in, a hard rain began to fall. "Great," I thought. I was just getting dry.

Old Blue sat there as the grand champion dog he was, he'd finished a mission that took years to complete. One-Eyed Jack had been a great adversary. He'd drowned more than one hunting dog and led others astray, there was not another dog that had got close to stopping him. But One-Eyed Jack had finally met his match. Old Blue never gave up, gave in or gave out. He learned One- Eyed Jack's tricks and made up his mind that he would never get the best of him again.

One-Eyed Jack tried everything to stop Old Blue. He walked up and down trees, through holes and through streams trying to throw Old Blue off and for a while it worked. But he didn't plan on Old Blue never giving up. All the screaming that One-Eyed Jack was doing was saying *How in the world did you figure it out!*

There wasn't a dog in ten counties that could do what Old Blue had done. He had a plan, no matter what he followed it through. Old Blue's journey was filled with disappointment and despair. He'd faced the pain of the forest, briar patches and more obstacles than any human could count. That first night he'd made the saddest sound I'd ever heard a dog make. But it was the battle, the pain, the disappointment and his will to win that made him more than a conqueror, a grand champion hunting dog.

When you begin to change your life, you'll lose a few battles. But it's the fight and the pain that helps you win the war. If you fight determined to win shaking off the past and focusing on the present and always believing, you'll be receiving.

The devil has drowned more than one person's dreams and led thousands astray, but he'll meet his match with God as your guide. No matter what obstacles he puts in your way. God will help you learn his tricks, and his diversions. You need to encompass persistence, patience, and power working an unstoppable plan no matter what lies behind or ahead. You'll dictate and dominate over anything the devil throws at you. And achieve what you believed. It will be hard for him to ever get the best of you again.

Submit yourselves therefore to God. Resist the devil, and he will flee from you

James 4:7

Not walk away but run away.

You may walk through the forest, and through obstacles few can overcome, and even think you're lost. But if you never give up, never surrender making God your guide, you'll find your way, the devil will be yelling *"How in the world did you figure this out!"*

There may be a lot of scary moments. There is real pain in life, bad relationships, bad luck and bad times. Sometimes It feels like you're finding more obstacles than you can overcome. You may cry, be sad and even depressed. But remember it's the battle, the pain and the disappointment that gives you the wisdom to become more than a conqueror. It may not be easy but when you finally walk away from the trap satan has set for you, you'll be amazed at what you've learned.

To eliminate strife, give God control of your life. Give God all your visions and dreams, He'll show you how to destroy the devil's tricks and schemes. Being led through this physical world by the spiritual person inside of you, gives the devil nowhere to hide.

What shall we say then to these things? If God is for us, who can be against us-

Romans 8:31

For as many as are led by the Spirit of God, they are the sons of God. For ye have not received the spirit of bondage again to fear; but ye have received the Spirit of adoption, whereby we cry, Abba, Father.

The Spirit itself beareth witness with our spirit, that we are the children of God: Nay, in all these things we are more than conquerors through him that loved us. For I am persuaded, that neither death, nor life, nor angels, nor principalities, nor powers, nor things present, nor things to come, nor height, nor depth, nor any other creature, shall be able to separate us from the love of God, which is in Christ Jesus our Lord.

Romans 8

When the Kingdom of God is within you, the devil will flee he can't take on that onslaught.

His only tactic is to whisper in your ear. If you listen he will discourage and defeat you but don't let him in, don't let him win.

It may seem at times that nothing is going your way, you feel your lost in a dark forest, by a dark river, and it begins to rain. You might want to give up or give in, but don't you dare, because it's in those times that you dust yourself off, stand up, and finish your plan. The knowledge and the strength you gain, is what leads to being free.

Growth comes when you battle win or lose; you gain insight for the next fight. You fight faster, harder and wiser. Understand that strength and resolve will allow you to win. If you will not weaken, give up or give in.

Old Blue was smarter and more driven than any hound in our county. He followed his plan every time he hunted. He became the most expensive and sought-after hunting dog in that whole Blue Ridge Mountain area.

What's your plan? Do you have one? Do you wake up in the morning letting life kick you around or do you wake up ready to hunt?

Do you want to win? Then surrender your old, defeating habits and renew your child-like heart. You can't gain with pain unless you train your brain to deal with the strain. If you're heavily burdened, you'll be blinded by the obstacles you face. Which will lead you astray as you lose your way.

When you walk outside the world greets you with the good, the bad and the ugly. You must find the secret of reaching within yourself to find the strength to carry on. Determination and adhering to a plan *"No matter what"* leads to a better day. To the completion of your dreams, your visions and your goals. Change is required…if what you are doing is not working, it's time to try something new.

REDVERB: Risk is a component of change and change is the main ingredient of growth. The speed of growth is determined by the amount of risk you're willing to take.

Getting back to the basics of life involves an unstoppable, unchangeable, unshakeable commitment to your plan. Every plan, no matter how big or small requires the ability to start with that first step. No matter the pain you've felt, the folks that have hurt you, or the things you've done to yourself, the past is gone. You can celebrate it, regret it, forget it or let it rule your life day by day. Or you can learn from it, turn from it, or discern from it. No matter what you decide to do, the past is a distant shore, you don't live there anymore.

It's time to leave the past behind and embrace the day. It's time to take that first step.

Isn't it time?

Isn't it time to look at yourself and leave behind the things that have stolen your dreams, your peace and your joy.

Old Blue taught me to never give up staying focused on what mattered. He'd been hurt it was evident by those scars. Scars can be deep enough to stop you from winning. Old Blue did something about his pain when he went back into that forest. He had every right to give up, but he didn't, he stayed committed to his goal, he found what he was looking for, total absolute victory.

The devil is your One-Eyed Jack. He has hurt and schemed against you leaving scars behind. He's killed some led astray thousands, even millions. Don't let him stop you.

You'll achieve what you believe and receive what you need. You're in a spiritual battle for your very soul fighting a wily opponent; who engages his plan and deceptions daily in your life. The devil plans and implements his schemes as a skilled opponent making it hard to get through the obstacles he's put in your way.

He has a plan, do you? His plan is to have you walk through briar patches, through streams, searching through old logs and brush to make sure your lost. It's hard to find your way if you're not prepared for the hunt. Your "**ENEMY**" the devil, will win if you don't head him off at the pass.

It's time to get serious about your life because the devil is serious about taking yours. His plan? To keep you in a state of worry, pain and fear, robbing you of any chance of becoming a kid again. Jesus won this battle, He tore up the devil. But the devil is wily he'll tell you nothing has changed, and if you listen he'll win.

What should you do? *"Let go and Let God"* walls will fall, chains will break, healing happens, and the prison door will open. By letting God fight your battles you'll arrive in a place that is indescribable. A place where joy is powerful, and love is multiplied. A place where hope constitutes reality and peace is never ending.

Jesus is your mighty warrior He brought satan to his knees don't you let him stand up again. Convincing you that he has the power. Keep him where Jesus put him, because if he gets a toehold he will get a foothold and you'll be in a battle for your life. Invite Jesus to help He is a mighty warrior and has the scars to prove it.

Who his own self bares our sins in his body on the tree that we, being dead in our sins, should live unto righteousness: by whose stripes ye are healed.

1 Peter 2:24

Jesus was so confident about your future that He said to Peter:

And I also say unto thee, that thou art Peter, and upon this rock, I will build my church, and the gates of hell shall not prevail against it.

Matthew 16:18

What you believe becomes what you will be. If you think you'll make it, you're right. But on the other hand, if you think you won't make it then your also right. It's what you believe that makes your dreams either die in your life or fly in your life.

What Jesus did set you free to live a life full of unimaginable joy. He fought an incredible battle securing your peace with the ability to outdo any plans the devil had for you. When it seemed, all was lost, it looked like Jesus had lost His way as they took Him off the cross and buried Him. It looked like the devil your One-Eyed Jack had won. But three days later God's plan was revealed which to this day makes the devil scream, he caused it to happen but never figured it out until it was too late.

Develop a Plan

Don't let anyone steal your joy, your dreams or your vision. Joy is on the way, peace is nearby, and hope is right around the corner as you take that first step towards God as His love encompasses you.

Here's the question, do you want overwhelming joy or overburdened depression? Do you want the peace that passes all understanding or pain that produces ultimate fear? Do you want to know the power of love or the emptiness of a life unfulfilled? You can have anything you want if you follow the plan until you've found that meadow in the woods.

Old Blue enjoyed the rest of his life. He was more peaceful than I'd ever seen him. He'd journeyed, fought, and found the ultimate path that led to the fulfillment of defeating all the plans One-Eyed Jack had made. He believed he should, he believed he could, and he knew without a doubt that he would find his way.

Sitting under that old oak tree that night with the full moon shining around him, I swore Old Blue had earned a pair of wings. It was the first time I ever saw a dog smile. He'd found an incredible peace, he'd finished his course and completed his mission.

As you walk this new path leave the past behind to make room for a better future. You may be tempted to quit. But don't until you have found your way.

It's time to forgive those who've hurt you or abused you. Stay with your plan no matter what others say or the devil puts in your way. When you see that stream ahead, forge it, or an old log climb it. When you run through a few briar patches and feel some pain remember it will heal. Know that these obstacles are there to deceive you. The devil will try his best. He has lots of tricks up his sleeve.

But like any magician will tell you, it's just a diversion, a trick, a slight of hand designed to make you quit.

If you want to be a kid again, you need to get back the place when life was more fun than riding shotgun on the graham cracker and milk wagon in the first grade. It's time to enjoy life. A time of waking up, finding new friends, having adventures and finding new ways to play. Enjoying the moment, learning something new, getting out of your comfort zone. Then include the power of good friends, a good local church and a network of folks who are traveling down the same road you are.

And if one prevails against him, two shall withstand him; and a threefold cord is not easily broken

Ecclesiastes 4:12

We need each other especially when the hunt gets desperate. Find your own Talert and have some fun! You'll get wet, even score a few cuts and bruises, but before long you'll have the devil up a tree.

That night, as Mr. Johnson lifted his gun to shoot One-Eyed Jack Old Blue ran over and bumped him. Mr. Johnson looked into Old Blue's eyes and lowered his gun. Old Blue started leaving the forest and we followed right behind. One-Eyed Jack quit screaming. There was nothing, but silence and that silence spoke an incredible truth. One-Eyed Jack had been utterly defeated and had given up. As far as I know, no one ever saw him again. Old Blue had finished what he'd come to do. He never gave up, gave in or gave out

REDVERB: The difference between *"I can't, and I won't"* is *"I can, and I will"* its life changing. **DON'T YOU EVER GIVE UP...**

Don't be afraid of dying, be afraid of not living **Red Devine**

YOUR 1ˢᵀ SECRET MISSION

1. **Let go off your past, live for today:** Release it, let it go. There's one person that regrets, unforgiveness and bitterness hurts and *"That's you."*

2. **Develop a Plan:** Understand that there'll be challenges along the way. Life with its twists and turns can be tough you'll have battles to fight. It's the battle through the haze that teaches you the secrets of life. God will teach you how to let go of those things you no longer need. God has a plan for you:

"For I know the plans I have for you," declares the Lord, "plans to prosper you and not to harm you, plans to give you hope and a future." Then you will call to me, and I will listen to you. You will seek me and find me when you seek me with all your heart.

Jeremiah 29:11-13

Open your arms to Him, allow Him in. He stands beside you to guide you and never lets you go. You are His joy, His greatest achievement. He is prouder of you than any Father can be. You should have a daily written plan to show your progress. Which leads to that clearing by the Old Oak Tree finding those answers you've been looking for.

3. **Change your world:** Don't let the world change you. Be a leader not a follower. Your mission is to develop your plan and stick

with it. Follow your dream, whatever it may be. Fulfilling your mission will lead to a pair of wings and a smile.

4. **Never Give UP...Never SURRENDER**...you'll find your way

These things I have spoken to you, that your joy might remain in you, and that your joy might be full.

John 15:11

Behold, I send you forth as sheep in the midst of wolves: be ye, therefore, wise as serpents, and harmless as doves.

Matthew 10:16

If a man knows not what harbor he seeks, any wind is the right wind. *Lucius Annaeus Seneca*

Children have neither a past nor a future; they enjoy the present, which very few of us do. *Jean de La Bruyere- Philosopher 1697*

The moment you doubt whether you can fly, you cease forever to be able to do it. *J.M. Barrie-Author of Peter Pan*

The devil destroys lives. God redeems hearts. The devil steals life, God gives life. The devil breeds hate, God is LOVE. What are you looking for?

Moment of Mirth: Contrary to popular belief, it wasn't the apple on the tree that got us banished from Paradise. It was the pair on the ground.

Task #1:

It's time to Hula -Hoop!

2

The Devil's Nickel

Alameda, California 1960

There was a loose board in the fence at Tony's convenience store near our apartments. My doorway to the outside world. I'd push hard getting through because dirt and debris would build up there. I was scraped by a nail or splinter but it was worth the price.

Tony's had been there for quite a while with its faded paint and glued on signs from concerts long ago. The pavement was old and cracked revealing years of wear, with spots blackened by old chewing gum and half-lit cigarettes that had been smashed till they no longer glowed. Through the front door to the right was the most important place on earth *"The candy section."* It was filled with all the necessities of life.

All most every day I'd pick up bottles, help folks out with chores, do everything I could to earn a nickel, my passport to this heavenly place. In the sixties it would buy a bag of candy. I learned what the word motivation meant. I was motivated to earn as many nickels as possible.

I didn't know my dad, he was always out to sea. I was five- years old and only remembered that when he was home nobody was happy. He was a sad, complicated, abusive, troubled man.

It wasn't long till my mother divorced him. So, it was up to my mom and I to make sure our house was kept up. Being a good kid, at least I thought so, my mom would give me a new shiny nickel to spend at Tony's. This particular day she reached in her purse and handed me my passport to heaven. The penny candy was calling me. Little did I know this was going to be the most unusual day in my young life.

In seconds I had my shoes on running faster than a cheetah on speed, faster than the Flash. I'm surprised that my tennis shoes didn't burn up.

There was a grass field between our apartment and the fence next to Tony's. I had great memories there, spending hours playing with my friends, climbing the big tree in the middle of the field. At night we would watch movies at the drive-in just down the street. When the wind blew the branches apart it would give us time to fire our cannons at the British. We were pirates on a great adventure. Or detectives looking for clues to a crime that no one could solve. We couldn't hear the movies, so we'd write our own scripts. Playing different parts, at times laughing so hard we'd almost fall out of the tree.

As I ran towards the grass field there was no sign of Johnny Allen, my co-conspirator on many a pirate's voyage. He would've known I scored and even though a nickel could buy a bay of candy, it didn't go far when two of us was eating it.

It was a beautiful day in northern California. The nickel in my hand felt secure as I ran towards the old fence by the highway with the green field in front of me. I started going through a list of all the penny candies that were there. Lost in thought I was half way across the grass when something awful happened.

My hand was empty, I'd lost my nickel. I panicked, looking for my nickel like it was pure gold, lifting my feet, going to my knees, parting the grass and digging in the ground. The thought of losing my nickel was more than I could bare. How could this have happened?

I was determined to find it. I traced my steps back towards our apartment, with each step I grew more anxious, I couldn't find my nickel! How would I ever live again?

Suddenly something happened, and it was beyond belief. You see I'd never been to church in my life. My folks were not what you might call *"Church People."* No one ever talked about God much less the devil. But I had a feeling that someone was always watching over me. I had no idea who He was I just felt he was always there.

I looked frantically in my shoes and the grass around me but to no avail my nickel was gone. There was no nickel. My life as I knew was over.

But then right in front of me something strange began to happen. The ground began to boil up from underneath, splitting the field open. At first, I thought it was a gopher or some other kind of animal, but it was much scarier, a gnarly hand came up from the ground and in its grasp, was my new, shiny nickel.

I watched helplessly as my nickel disappeared when the hand went back into the earth. I jumped up trying to grab my nickel but as soon as it had appeared, it disappeared. Something inside of me said *"It was the devil's hand!"* The devil had stolen my nickel, whoever he was. It was so real I'd stood up backing away. I was wondering what in the world was going on. And then it hit me here was a new enemy in my life. This dirty, rotten devil had stolen my nickel taking away my dreams. As furious as a kid could be, I stamped the earth trying to close the ground where the gnarly hand had been. I stood tall and shook my finger yelling loudly, *"devil, you're going to pay for stealing my nickel. You should have picked on someone else! I'll get my nickel back!"*

I walked home, dejected and forlorn. When I got home my mom saw that I had no candy, so she asked what had happened, I shared my story of how the devil had stolen my nickel. She laughed and said that was the best story she had ever heard. As time passed, I'd walk back to the same spot, looking for my nickel, carrying my Red Rider BB gun for protection. I must have scared him because he never showed up again. It seemed that the devil was a little worried about what a five-year old kid might do. Little did he know from that day forward, he was in for a fight.

Show me your faith without deeds, and I will show you my faith by what I do. You believe that there is one God. Good! Even the demons believe that and shudder.

James 2:18

Where does the stress, the pain, and the darkness come from? It can seem overwhelming at times. Life has a habit of wearing us down and tearing us apart. This isn't God's plan but the devil's delight. He loves watching you crumble and fall. He employs his three little thieves, worry, depression and fear specializing in stealing your joy, peace and your love. He's the father of all liars.

Then said Jesus to those Jews which believed on him, if ye continue in my word, then are ye my disciples indeed; And ye shall know the truth, and the truth shall make you free. (Talking to the Jews who were seeking to destroy Him) *Ye are of your father the devil, and the lusts of your father ye will do. He was a murderer from the beginning, and abode not in the truth, because there is no truth in him. When he speaketh a lie, he speaketh of his own: **for he is a liar, and the father of it.** And because I tell you the truth, ye believe me not.*

John 8:31-47

These criminals sent by a mastermind rob you of every gift you had as a child. Weapons put into place to help you survive in a very dark world. Without them, you're like a bird with broken wings trying to rise above the turbulence of your frustrations staying grounded with every predator looking your way. Lost no way to find your way home, depressed, bound and fearful, watching your plans become shattered by unknown forces.

Children have an unvarnished view of the world. Their hearts full of love and compassion they see the world differently than adults. This gives them the ability to have an incredible amount of faith, unstoppable love and forgiveness even if they were abused or forgotten.

The tough things that have happened to you can feel orchestrated. You sense that someone else is pulling the strings, putting obstacles in your way, some very destructive. Some families find themselves living in disarray and misery experiencing the worst of life from generation to generation, leading to a family tradition of defeat and despair. Which is their inheritance that every member of the family is rewarded without going to probate court.

You have a choice, unfortunately, that's why evil inhabits your world. Some embrace the darkness, fighting an endless battle without any useable weapons. Pushed around by every wind. While others have equipped themselves for battle by gaining the spiritual weapons that come from inhabiting and living in the light. With God as their partner, they are not alone and have the weapons needed to secure victory. If you choose darkness the devil will play you, without God there's no power strong enough to save you.

As the light is switched on things become clearer because light always overcomes darkness. If you stand in a dark room next to a doorway leading into a lighted room, that light will enter through any small crevice and illuminate the darkest room. Light always overcomes the darkness.

The Darkened Room

You're trapped in a dark room and notice that light is trying to get in. You wonder what's on the other side, you reach for the doorknob, trying to escape the darkness you're in. Caressing the door knob, you hold tight, and try to turn it. But as you do from out of nowhere there are sounds in the darkness that you cannot identify; it's important to find the light, your heart beats wildly.

Your hand feels the coolness of the metal doorknob, you twist it, it feels locked, you panic. You turn the knob it won't move, the sounds and the darkness now encase you and the hair on the back of your neck stands up, a cold chill fills the room. It's imperative that you find the light, you need to escape the darkness. Your hand slips. You let go of the door falling back into the room. Fear sets in as darkness is all you can feel, you need to find that door, but you're frozen with fear. A presence wraps its boney fingers around your heart, you dare not open your eyes.

You know that the light is where you need to be. You feel your way back to the door you grab the door knob once again. You turn it and as you pull the door it sticks; you push against it, but it barely moves. There is now a definite presence in the room; you can sense it. You feel its cold breath as it tries to pull you back in. A low terrifying voice speaks *"Why try?"* More ungodly voices fill the room, they sound familiar; you've felt this presence and heard these voices before.

You pause for a moment loosening your grip, you're tired and weary from fighting, maybe the voice is right, *"Why try?"* But something pushes you forward you can sense the darkness leaving when the voices begin to fade. Then you see the it, the light, it's warmth and comfort can be felt. The voices drift further away. Calamity and the darkness have tried to hold you; they tugged at your heart, But, then you give it one more try and with every fiber in your being you pull and slam the door wide open.

The door bounces off the wall, the sound echoing throughout the room. It leaves an impression in the sheetrock and as you fall to your knees, the tears cascade down your face, enveloping the sweat that made the door so hard to open.

The dust from the broken sheetrock shines like tiny stars in the light that frees you. It lands on you and envelopes you with its warmth empowering you. Something deep inside comes alive the light vanquishes the darkness. It desperately runs from its brilliance but to no avail.

The light consumes the darkness; the fearsome babbling and negative voices cease, the darkness flees, you have a sense of calm and a presence of peace that brings harmony and balance to your spirit. The unrelenting fear that you felt eases. Faith replaces it as the light reveals the truth.

The darkness runs away like a fast train on greased wheels headed down a mountainside of ice powered by a 454-turbo charged engine pushed by a jet stream, hell bent to find a dark place to hide, you can see clearly every corner of your room. There is no place to hide because the light has now encompassed the darkness.

The great deceiver is a conniver and a master liar. He'll tell you that failure is your only option. The voices you hear say *"Change is not good. Don't leave the comfort of the darkness that you've grown accustomed to! Have you thought about what's on the other side?*

Are you sure you want to go there? Remember failure, and regret and all the other times you tried? We can do this on some other day, can't we?"

As the light enters the room, there's an immediate release of power that makes the devil shiver as he hurries and scurries away. Things in your life start to fall into place you begin to understand just how dark it was. The devil's only defense is to convince you that nothing's changed, the room is still dark. And if you listen to him long enough, you might believe him.

As he employs his schemes and lies, he hopes that you'll close your eyes to the truth. If you do, he becomes embolden by your actions and starts dimming the lights once again. His greatest fear is that you'll realize your full potential and see him as he is, out of the shadows and into the light.

He understands the power of light. His only hope is that you'll never comprehend what has just happened.

He knows that you can now see the shadows. Your fear is gone, your joy has returned. You're no longer worried because the light has illuminated the darkness.

I was made aware that darkness existed, very early in life. Which led me to forgive those who had been played by the devil themselves. When I walked out of the darkness I became aware of who was "*Pulling the strings*" from the shadows. God's word, provided the most impressive, overwhelming, incredible, powerful and fantastic truth that severed those strings completely. All of it drawn from the light cascading from the Kingdom of God.

Your enemy is not your parents, your friends or anyone else in your life. I watched the enemy destroy my family, kept my mom and dad in chaos, stole our joy and peace. We walked in the light we were given and stumbled a lot in some very dark places.

You need to quit blaming your parents, your family and the friends you have. The devil's best deception is to convince you that it was them; it was always them. If only I had been treated different, maybe even loved, I could have succeeded.

You will succeed, and you will be different by realizing the truth and abiding in it.

REDVERB: You either affect life or it affects you. You must control your life, or it will control you. You either follow or lead. If you're not the lead dog the view never changes.

Many people have suffered and bled on the field of battle who eventually became champions despite their past or any abuse they may have encountered. They decided to not let life change them but to change the life around them. satan will keep you off balance and weak if you let him as he uses every trick and deception possible. If you listen to him, he will win. It's impossible to be a kid again carrying the weight of the world on your shoulders.

The Bible says:

The devil has come to kill, steal and destroy.

He roams the earth like a lion seeking whom he may devour.

John 10:10-1 Peter 5:8

Pretty brutal; it doesn't take long to look at the world and see that he has been very busy. He's not your friend and doesn't care if you live or die. In fact, he is overjoyed to see you live in despair and pain.

There is hope and light for all. Things change as you enter the Kingdom of Light. The only power he possesses is the power you give him.

He's a powerless deceiver and if you believe his lies he will gain power over you. But once you walk in the light as He is in the light, your life changes. Now the Kingdom of Light is within you.

It's important to stay in the light. You can't see shadows in the dark. It's the shadows that robbed you of the gift's you had as a child. The shadows of night steal your joy and your ability to play. When you abide in the light, darkness has nowhere to hide.

And once the light gives you the freedom you've always wanted then joy becomes a weapon, peace a place of strength realizing that love is the most powerful force on earth. God is love. Understanding love is when you understand God.

Never let the devil steal your joy.

"The Joy of the Lord is our (your) strength"

Nehemiah 8:10

Why do you think he works hard to convince you that joy is lost, and things will never change? He knows where your strength lies.

Change your panic attack into a plan of attack. Once you enlist in God's *"Light Brigade"* it teaches you the path to complete and total victory. It's a journey, if you never give up, never give in and never give out, you'll complete your quest. Freedom will be your reward

REDVERB: Things change overnight, as you fight, with all your might, for the right, to stay in the light.

You accomplish this embracing a child's faith, a child's heart by letting go and letting God. The deceiver wants to steal all the weapons you received as a child by grinding the joy right out of you. He's hoping you'll drop the weapon of joy and give up any idea of peace. As he reaches inside your heart and snatches your greatest weapon, "love."

He seeks to steal any hope of being a kid again leading you to a pathway of hopelessness. As you grasp for air hoping to repair what's left of a broken life. Taking your most powerful weapons and replacing them with counterfeit items that are powerless. If you give in you will weaken and submit to his ways. Where there is no escape. Locked in a lifestyle that becomes your personal hell.

"For we wrestle not against flesh and blood, but against principalities, against powers, against the rulers of darkness of this world, against spiritual wickedness in high places.

Ephesians 6:12

As you walk in the Light, you'll feel a powerful presence that won't leave you even in your darkest hours. His presence is close beside you. It's His presence no matter how tough the battle may seem will help you hold onto the weapons you received as a child.

Children are born with an unshakeable faith, a remarkable love. Even when tested most children believe that things will get better.

God will not let you down. If you wander while you're seeking answers in the darkness, you'll feel Him as close as a whisper and as powerful as a hurricane wind. He'll wrap His arms around you, hold you and never let you go if you allow Him to.

True freedom comes when you learn to forgive. No matter what pain may be in your past. There's freedom when you realize who's behind the pain and suffering you've experienced. The enemy's plan is the opposites of God's. Where there is love, he brings hate and where there's faith, he brings fear.

If there is peace in the house, he brings division through the front door. He'll reach right into your heart and steal your hope, and any love you had. Watching your weapons drop to the floor defenseless and vulnerable.

You'll fall victim to his conniving ways. If you live without God, then you're playing into the devil's hands. He'll hurt you, desert you and destroy you. The physical world is his playground and if you play in his sand you'll get buried.

Walking in the light is the first step to becoming a brand-new creature.

Therefore, if any man be in Christ, he is a new creature: old things are passed away; behold, all things are become new.

2 Corinthians 5:17

You are now something else for the devil to deal with. God is the hydrogen bomb to the devil's firecracker. Your faith grows, your love multiplies, and you are empowered walking in the light.

The world is now a place of opportunity and joy, where success and healing become a reality. Seeing the world through God's eyes brings peace to a troubled heart. It's the devil's turn to pack his bag and leave on an extended trip away from you. The devil's greatest weakness is he lives in the same world he created. He abides in fear and depression with no hope of love.

With no God to save him. Lonely in his despair he tries to snare you in the same trap he finds himself in. Misery loves company. When you walk into the Kingdom of Light you gain powers that Superman wished he had. You'll be able to do more than just leap tall buildings in a single bound. The day you become one hundred percent spirit led and accept God in His fullness, mountains will crumble, weapons will cease to fire. And life becomes a place of peace and understanding.

It's the gateway to the garden where you play unhindered, a kid's paradise. Full of joy, where love solves all things.

As a child I learned about this idiotic, powerless, stupid fool the devil. I learned that my real battle was with him.

The threat I made as a five-year-old kid must have resonated in hell, because I've found nickels in the strangest places wherever I've traveled. Never dimes or quarters, just nickels. In San Diego I saw a nickel on an elevator sign. I've found nickels on streets, walkways even in churches. It's my goal to reveal the true nature and weakness of the devil. No matter how many times he's tried to give me my nickel back I refuse his bribery.

There are many names for the devil. Beelzebub, satan, lucifer, some call him the ugly old devil others just call him "life." Even if you don't believe in spiritual warfare, God or the devil, one thing you must admit evil is kicking and screaming around the world.

Evil is not a simple thing it's a hugely influential force, a living organism. If you give it life it will bring death to your dreams your hopes and eventually to your future. No matter what you call this force or what you envision him to be you need to make a choice of where your allegiance falls. If you chose the darkness he will teach you hate. Hate is something you learn. The devil wrote the book *"Hatred for Dummies"* and he'll give you lessons any time you ask.

One of my favorite songs goes like this: *"You may be an Ambassador to England or France, you might like to gamble, you might like to dance, you may be the heavyweight champion of the world or a socialite with a long string of pearls. But you have to serve somebody, it may be the devil, or it may be the Lord, but you have to serve somebody."*

Life is simple. What you sow you reap. If you feel unloved find someone that needs love. Help them become a better version of themselves. It's the act of giving of yourself that will heal any broken heart you may have!

No one is responsible for your daily personal pain. Someone may have brought you to a place of sorrow, but if you're not careful, you'll continue to carry that pain to your grave. Yes, someone did it to you. Yes, they were the ones that started the conflict in your soul. But they are not carrying the weight of that burden you carry. If you walk in fear, grow faith. If you live in depression, then you need to reach out to those that live in the shadows and help bring them to the light. That will help you see the bright path ahead.

You must make up your mind that things will be different. You need to make that decision.

No matter how good I am at writing or your pastor at preaching or Oprah's show is at revealing, if you don't find a way to a better day, then nothing ever changes. I can't change you, God can't change you. Your family or your friends can't change you. The only person that will allow you to change is *"YOU."*

REDVERB: Understanding the truth will light the fire of your desire to take you higher, out of the mire. It will require you to take a different path.

The revelation that the devil is the author of most of your pain helps you understand that the closer you get to the light, the further away he runs from you taking the darkness with him.

Comprehending who your real enemy is makes all the difference. He stole your childhood, brought pain and destruction into your life and family, maybe even took away someone you loved. He uses his sleight of hand to steal. His goal is to take your nickel and never give it back again. He creates pain and death. The death of your dreams, your visions, your life. Drawing you into a world of confusion and despair.

The devil had a plan for you the day you were born. To strip you from any belief in the impossible, by showing you the unbelievable and the so-called unworkable problems in life. He whispers his lies and deceptions hoping you will listen. His intention is to convince you to give up and give in. But there is good news.

Ye are of God, little children, and have overcome them: because greater is he that is in you, than he that is in the world.

1 John 4:4

It's time to reclaim that which has been lost, to become a kid again.

A time when you believed in the miraculous, when everything and anything seemed possible.

Always having an overwhelming faith that we could fly. It's time to gather your gifts, your weapons for fighting this dark force. Love is the most powerful weapon against hate. Faith is an unstoppable power that destroys worry and depression. Peace comes when joy takes place of sadness.

God gave you an imagination to allow you to create beautiful dreams and visions. The devil uses imagination to create worry, hoping to steal those dreams. Worry is the misuse of your imagination. If you fall into this trap, you will worry about things that haven't even happened yet. Setting your mind free to create solutions instead of problems will help you secure your new-found weapons of life.

REDVERB: There are no such things as problems, just solutions.

Worry is the misuse of your imagination.

The attributes of these gifts were given to you as a child allowing you to power through life. That's why the deceiver works so hard to steal them. He puts you in situations where you'll give up your gifts.

Instead of living in joy, you accept fear, pain or depression as a replacement. These counterfeit items are the gifts he rewards you with as you hand over your joy. *"DON'T"* ever let the devil or any person on earth or in the heavens above steal your joy!

Your imagination was intended to fulfill your dreams, to enable you to imagine how beautiful your world can be. Imagination is an incredible force that can bring joy into your life, or a place the devil goes to steal, kill and destroy any hope for your future.

What would happen if your reality was immediately shaped by your imagination. Use it incorrectly and your bills overwhelm you and it becomes true. Imagine you're getting promoted and the next day you start believing you're headed towards that corner office. Imagine your marriage failing apart or imagine a marriage coming together full of joy and fulfilling love they both can become true it depends on what you imagine to be true. Imagination is the precursor to reality.

What would your life become if you lived the life you imagined?

In your fight with this evil, dark opponent it's important to realize that your family, your friends, your bosses none of these are your enemies. The devil will use them to try and destroy you but always remember who your real enemy is.

Everyone makes mistakes. Some have a lot to give while others have little to share. You can only expect people to give what they can.

No one understands the world as you do. That's like expecting a baby to do calculus. Even though you may be able to do calculus in your sleep. A baby can't find convergence because of decreasing function they have no idea of what you're doing. Exponential growth and function come from a harmonic sequence that is dedicated to the higher derivative and includes Integration maximized by God's unending love. Don't expect others to have the same talents or abilities that you have.

As Bishop Jakes has said "*Some people are pint people, and some are quart people.*" Some just have more to give than others. It helps you comprehend why some people do what they do. Don't put unrealistic expectations on those who are not there yet.

Fight the good fight, focus on your real enemy. The best path to peace is to forgive those who have harmed you stealing your dreams and visions. Learning to forgive leads to the fantastic secrets of love. It's a brand-new day when you realize who is really behind all that pain. It's a brand- new life when you unpack the past and move forward to a powerful, positive imagined future.

REDVERB: Life is not about finding yourself. It's about creating yourself.

You can become *"**The You**"* you want to be. Give yourself a break no one is perfect, and you never will be. Seeking perfection is one of the devil's favorite weapon's. He knows that you will destroy your life and those around you by expecting perfection.

Strive to do the best you can. Failure is only a door-way to understanding life on a new level, learning from that failure. Strive for excellence in everything you do. The challenge is to see yourself as God sees you, as His grand and beautiful child. He loves you not because of what you can do but of who you are. His gifts include patience, mercy and forgiveness because He knew you would need them. Not only for yourself but to use in dealing with others.

God's love is unimaginable, unbelievable and unchangeable.

He wants to give you an unstoppable supply of gifts. As you take one He's busy wrapping the next one just hoping you're ready to receive it. The only thing that stops him is that you've not used the one He's given you. With your hands full there's no way to receive another.

Receive the gift.

Failure happens when we don't act. When we can't change, or not willing to. Your life will go nowhere if you're not willing to go anywhere. You need to take the time to open the gift that's been given to you.

Every great action starts with one step. The first step is the hardest to take. Some problems are so ingrained in your life it's hard to even try. But once you take that first step the second one is easier. It helps to find a friend, a church, a pastor or program that will help you support your new life in the light. Find them and be patient with yourself.

Self-hatred becomes a self-defeating process. You must believe in yourself. How can you expect others to believe in you if you don't believe in you? You could have taken hurtful words of another to heart. They can be destructive, but you have the right to receive them or turn them away. Many times, the things that are said and done to you or motivated by someone else's problems and situations. It really may have nothing to do with you at all.

To become a kid again you need to enjoy who and what you are. Never give into the bullies in your life don't give them permission to steal your joy. When you fight back a bully they'll usually run away. Love who and what you are and what you are becoming.

Create fun, share love, release joy these weapons once used will kick the devil right back to where he belongs.

Life will begin to change, and you will start finding a few nickels of your own. Give all your cares, burdens, lost dreams and disappointments to God. He's good at turning all that into pure, fantastic, mighty fun recharging your childlike heart. Eliminate those folks in your life who see nothing but darkness they can bump into some dangerous places and take you with them. It's the light that illuminates your way.

For you were once darkness, but now you are light in the Lord. Live as children of light...for it is the light that makes everything visible

Ephesians 5: 8-14

Thy word is a lamp unto my feet, and a light unto my path

Psalm 119:105

It takes faith to move ahead. The path can seem dangerous and dark. But God promises if you take that first step He will light up the next one. You just need a small amount of faith to take that first step.

Remember the devil does not play fair make sure it is God who is leading the way. He will help you fight the battles ahead and keep you on the path that leads to a better day.

Once you come to terms with your spiritual self, God's kingdom and His power are within you. Not only to fight the battle but to win the war. Isn't it time to turn the TV off - *The Bachelorette* will survive without you.

Here's more power for the journey:

You, dear children, are from God and have overcome them, because the one who is in you is greater than the one who is in the world

I John 4:4

Humble yourselves therefore under the mighty hand of God, that he may exalt you in due time: Casting all your care upon him; for he careth for you. Be sober, be vigilant; because your adversary the devil, as a roaring lion, walketh about, seeking whom he may devour:

1 Peter 5:6-8

And do not give the devil a foothold

Ephesians 4:27

…The reason the Son of God appeared was to destroy the devil's work.

1 John 3:8

The thief comes only to steal and kill and destroy; I have come that you may have life to the full.

John 10:10

Finally, be strong in the Lord and in His mighty power. Put on the full armor of God so that you can take your stand against the devil's schemes. For our struggle is not against flesh and blood, but against rulers, against the authorities, against the powers of this dark world

Ephesians 6:10-11

Submit yourselves, then, to God. Resist the devil, and he will flee from you. Come near to God and He will come near to you

James 4:7-8

YOUR 2ND SECRET MISSION

1. Have a Plan

2. Realize that you have an enemy

3. Fight for the right, to stay in the light, life will be out of sight
   (In other words darkness kills, light reveals)

Your life has been impacted by an evil force, a force dedicated to make you quit, give up, give in or give out. The deceiver's real power comes into play when you succumb to his temptations and the plans he's made for you. His plan is to tie you up in the negative things of this world keeping you from being the person God designed you to be. Full of power and unrelenting love.

Dreams don't come true living the devil's nightmares. If you've decided to play in the devil's playground you have the freewill to do so. But you'll find out that there is a lot more terrifying things there than just the monkey bars.

The devil gets his power by conning you into believing his lies and mental deceptions. Your mind is the battle ground he fights in the only power he has is the power you give him.

Life can be a challenge when those around you bring home pain and suffering instead of joy and happiness. You have a lot to get over by how fast you can get from under it.

The devil worked against you before you were born. If you go back to past generations, you can see how his plans were rooted into your family tree. It branched out and encompassed everyone it touched, leaving its stain and despair. The word says that your battle is not against flesh and blood, but Spiritual.

For we wrestle not against flesh and blood, but against principalities, against powers, against the rulers of the darkness of this world, against spiritual wickedness in high places.

Ephesians 6:12

For the weapons of our warfare are not carnal, but mighty through God to the pulling down of strong holds;

2 Corinthians 10:4

Your mission if you decide to accept it is to not let the enemy get a toehold in your life. Become aware of the temptations and voices you hear. If the enemy gets a toehold he will soon get a foothold, and that becomes a *"stronghold"* and once he has that satan can pull you all the way in. The greatest defense you have is the Word of God. It's what Jesus used to overcome the devil's temptations in His life.

When the devil would tempt him, Jesus would say *"It is written."*

Stand your ground and the fog will clear, the weapons he uses against you will fail.

No weapon that is formed against thee shall prosper; and every tongue that shall rise against thee in judgment thou shalt condemn. This is the heritage of the servants of the Lord, and their righteousness is of me, saith the Lord.

Isaiah 54:17

And on that clear day you will see forever. Jesus destroyed the devil's plans when he died was buried and rose again. This act took away all the power the devil had to destroy you. The only way the devil can resurrect that power is if you give him permission to do so. Never forget that the full power of the realm of God lives within you the awesome, incredible, unbelievable. Unstoppable, miracle-generating, life changing power of God's kingdom is within you once you accept Him into your life. You have the authority through Jesus Christ to make the devil run away like a banshee on fire.

REDVERB: Believe, achieve, perceive as you conceive and receive this new life.

"One of the virtues of being very young is that you don't let the facts get in the way of your imagination"

Sam Levenson

"In my soul, I am still a small child who did not care about anything else but the beautiful colors of a rainbow."

Papiha Ghosh

Moment of Mirth: Advise from Kids

Never trust a dog to watch your food or never dare your little brother to paint the family car, when you want something expensive, ask your grandparents. Never try to baptize the cat. And when your dad is mad and asks, *"Do I look stupid?"* don't answer him. Never spit on a roller coaster and don't ever be too full for desert.

Task #2: Buy a Yo-Yo and learn three new tricks with it.

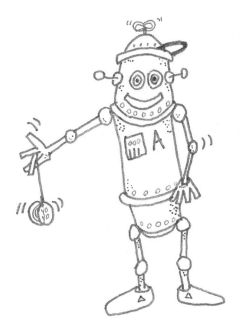

CHAPTER

3

Sandals on the sand

The air was dry, the dust flying as hundreds of people pressed in to see Him. The sun shone bright in the afternoon sky making it difficult to see, but the sounds of sandals shifting on the sand could clearly be heard.

High above the town, ravens circled the sky looking for a chance meal or a good place to land. The sun reflected off their wings like black mirrors as the heat of the day caused them to rise and fall, shifting with the changing currents of the wind. They chattered constantly discussing the day's events. They circled slowly flying lower to get a closer look.

As they did, they could hear the people yelling out His name. Voices rang out from every corner, overcoming the ravens loud piercing comments. A cacophony of blurred words and requests followed at every step He took. *"Jesus! Over here! I need to be healed."*

"Hey Jesus, bless me!" There was as many needs as the sand that they walked on. Everyone was yelling out His name. *"Jesus, what about me?"*

He heard everyone, their need was far more than physical. As He calmly walked through the crowd they reached out to touch Him to be near Him. They knew that His presence could heal, and His words would help. He fostered love, preaching peace while He unfolded faith.

This man Jesus was different.

They followed as He taught. So, did miracles and changed lives, His spirit pure. Passing by they felt it. He wore love like a never-ending cloak. When He spoke the storms and the unrelenting seas obeyed Him. The waves of uncertainty and pain that filled their lives gave way to a peacefulness that was hard to explain. Everything He did stilled the storm.

His love invaded their hearts calming any personal battle they were fighting. Everywhere He went was a major event. Casting out demons by the hundreds, healing folks by the thousands. It's no wonder that Jesus became the center of their world and ours today.

This overwhelming gift of love and wisdom that He possessed was beyond belief. He shared a radical message, speaking of commitment and love. His words piercing their hearts, healing their souls revealing a new truth and understanding of life. As He shared His knowledge they found the missing piece of the puzzle they'd been looking for. It was finally fitting together.

As He looked at you, a part of your being became connected to the compassion He held, tearing right through your conflicted soul. He could see, feel and heal any heart of pain.

When He stopped and reached out, He touched them softly with His hands and deeply with His words. They would stop and strain to hear every verb and vowel. A great hush would ensue, as His words rang out. Being near Him was like a cool summer night after a hot and humid day as a welcome breeze touched you, cooled you, and calmed you. You felt alive and knew you would never be the same again.

When He was walking through the crowd, He noticed a man sitting near a stone wall holding a small wooden bowl. It was evident that he was blind. His hands were rough, calloused and cracked, each crevice darker than the rest. He held firmly to his gnarled wooden staff stained from seeing miles of torment as he clicked his way through the cobblestone streets of the City of David.

Jesus stopped and spoke to him. When He did the blind man began to rise, stumbling at first, Jesus grasped his arm to steady him. The crowd sensing something was about to happen moved closer in anticipation. Jesus held him for a moment and then reached down. When He rose, He had mud in His hands which He placed in the blind man's eyes. Surprised, the blind man asked." *Who are you?"* Jesus answered, *"Your humble servant."*

Jesus sensed that he was a loving man who saw with his heart. The blind man was known in the village and had been blind since birth. He wondered at the words that Jesus spoke they were different and powerful. He felt the warmth and compassion in His voice. He sensed His amazing spirit.

Jesus backed away from the man and said, *"I know you have wished to see, go, wash your eyes in the pool of Siloam."* The blind man thought for a moment, conflicted feeling vulnerable. He knew the place he had spent many days there. The pool was outside the walls of the city fed by the Gihon spring for over seven hundred years. He knew it well.

Surprised by Jesus's directions, the blind man paused for a moment as he remembered the stories he'd heard about this man Jesus and the miracles that had followed Him. Putting his reluctance aside, he held tight to his worn, gnarly staff, gathering himself together. He began to move through the crowd, struggling through the maze of people that made the common pathways he was used seem foreign. He moved slowly with each step and wondered if this miracle could be possible. His staff held him up and as he reached a cobblestone path you could hear the familiar click, clack of his staff, echoing off the stone walls as he made his way through the crowd.

This drew the crowd into a frenzy as they turned and implored, "*What about me?*" The noise was deafening. The ravens now surprised by the loud requests flew back into the sky cackling at the commotion.

As he walked the blind man wondered, "*Is this for real?*" He picked up his pace in anticipation reaching for the walls to help him find his way. "*Could this Jesus be who they say He is?*"

It was hard for him to comprehend what it must be like to see. His mother had tried to explain colors to him. She would hold his hand as a child and say, "*Do you feel the warmth of my hand?*" He would shake his head "*no*" which his mother knew meant "*yes.*" "*That's red*" she would say. Then she would have him feel cool water and say that was blue. Then take him to a tree to feel the leaves "*That's green.*" She took a leaf from the tree handing it to him it was as smooth as leather. He imagined how beautiful they would be to see.

She wanted him to understand the colors of the world what an amazing moment this would be if he could finally see them. It was a joke in his town when he would venture towards a warm fire and sometimes say, "*I love the red!*"

He understood the concept of color but wondered what it would be like to see them. Growing anxious he picked up his pace close to falling at times. Something inside him felt red the thought of seeing was almost too much to bear. He felt a tear begin to form that fell to his feet, washing away the dust, leaving a small stain on his worn sandals. His foot caught a loose stone, stumbling as the dust began to rise. He stopped for a moment. He could hear the towns people doing their daily chores at the spring. He was close.

He began to run, the voices of the towns people now even closer. Just behind him a few Jewish priests showed up he could hear their constant chatter, they sounded like the ravens that flew overhead. They were quoting Jewish law desperately looking for a law that Jesus had broken.

He knew they were trouble, they were always trouble. But it didn't matter. He felt the compassion Jesus held in His heart, the warmth of His hands they were redder than any hands he could remember. Nothing would stop him. He moved faster to stay ahead of their constant complaining.

He fell more than once on his journey to the springs even though he had walked this way before.

Getting close to the spring, he clumsily knocked over a few bird cages in the market. The doves inside scattered and flew in different directions. The merchant watching him yelled out, *"Who is going to pay for this you, stupid old man!"* He followed the blind man tripping on one of the broken cages. He angrily shook the cage off his foot and resumed his goal of chasing the blind man, determined to make him pay.

The blind man barely heard him. Reaching the pool, he threw his staff to the side where it bounced off a nearby wall. Falling forward he buried his face in the cool blue. He began washing his eyes as Jesus had told him to ensure that all the mud was removed.

Exhausted from his rapid journey, he rolled over on his back, his face wet, scared to open his eyes. Full of fear and trepidation, he rubbed them, hoping to wake them up. He had to know, there had been a previous time when a magician's trick didn't work. He didn't want to be fooled again. He had felt that pain before.

He could wait no longer. Little by little, he opened his eyes. First a small slit, then wide open, nothing changed. All he saw was darkness.

He laid there feeling like an idiot. He reached into the pool to remove the dirt that had stuck to his wet hands. Even though healers and magicians had tried in the past he thought this time it would work. But it didn't, even though he had done everything Jesus told him to do.

The shopkeeper still perturbed by the mornings events was right behind him yelling, *"Move over, stupid old man!"* Stepping by his legs as he jumped to catch a dove that had been released by the blind man's exploits. He was trying hard to catch every dove as he ran back and forth from the pool to his tables. As he reached for a dove he fell again to everyone's amusement. Laughter rang out as he removed a broken cage from his head.

"He's right, I am just a stupid old man" thought the blind man as he reached for his staff, disappointed and forlorn. His hand gripped the familiar rough exterior of his old friend. He felt insecure without it. He tried to hold himself together, but his tears began falling fast.

Just then he remembered what Jesus had said your faith had to be the size of a mustard seed. He thought for a moment, holding tight to his staff, that had been his eyes, his way around. Silently lying there as his heart beat as he tried to catch his breath.

He had held a mustard seed they were tiny and smooth. As he sat up and pulled himself together he thought *"Faith that small can do something this big?"* He wiped away the tears from his eyes as he began to rise.

Then something strange happened. His tears had washed away all the residue of the mud, a sharp massive bolt of light struck him. It was so powerful that it drove him to his knees dropping his staff. He couldn't move. Afraid of this new feeling, he tried to understand what had happened. It was like a dusty mirror had been wiped off he could sense light. Little by little he opened his eyes wide but was blinded by its intensity. He found the light difficult to comprehend as shapes began to come into focus.

Beside him was his worn haggard staff. It was both strange and familiar. He grasped it holding it to his chest. He felt secure. He rose holding tightly to it when a scary gray blurry thing came near him, it cooed. He was relieved it was a dove he had heard their call before.

The shopkeeper tried to catch the dove shouting, *"Move away old man!"* The blind man now seeing the shopkeeper for the first time reached over as he rose lifting him up, the shopkeeper's feet dangling in the wind.

The blind man spoke through his tears *"I caaaan see, I can see!"* he mumbled in disbelief. He hugged the shopkeeper who was trying to escape but to no avail. The blind man began to dance with him.

The befuddled shopkeeper couldn't believe his eyes he knew the man had been blind since birth.

The blind man tossed the shopkeeper around as he sung and praised God. He fell to his knees still holding tight to the shopkeeper, *"Praise God with me my friend!"* as he sang his praises to God. The shopkeeper pried himself loose standing a few feet away he wondered, *"What just happened?"* Speechless, not wanting to show any emotion, he backed against a nearby wall and quickly wiped away the tears that were beginning to form in his eyes. *"How is this possible?"*

He tried to make sense of it all, it was more than he could bear. He moved further away trying to grasp this miracle. *"If you can see, then help me catch my doves!"* he said weakly, trying to hide the tears that now flowed freely.

Overwhelmed by the colors that now surrounded the blind man his tears fell like rain. He began wiping away the tears as fast as he could he didn't want anything to keep him from seeing the red, the blue and green. He saw what he thought was a mustard plant. He reached down and held its soft green leaves and began to laugh. He couldn't wait to see his mother.

Blinded by the bright afternoon sun he rose and began to walk carrying his familiar staff. It was confusing and beautiful. He stopped by the pool and reached down to touch the water seeing it for the very first time. The sparkling rays of the sun ignited it changing the colors as it slipped through his hands. He started splashing the water like a child as it flew hitting the ground all around him. He could feel his heart begin to calm down as he rose. He had to find Jesus.

Leaving his staff behind, he walked over to a beautiful green tree. With a slow, deliberate breath, he took a leaf to hold onto. His clothes now drenched from playing in the water. Everything his mother said was true. He now felt and saw the colors amazed by their beauty.

His eyesight focused he reached down and picked up a small dove. In the past he had only known it's sound, he held it close, it was the most beautiful thing he had ever seen. He opened his eyes wider trying to see everything at once. To the chagrin of the shopkeeper, he raised his hands and watched the dove fly away, free to join his brothers in the sky, *"You'll pay for that you fool!"* His voice now quieter. Because it's hard to be mad in the middle of a miracle.

The blind man's laughter rang out as his tears continued to flow. What miracle was this? And who was this Jesus? He stumbled away from the tree, giving the shopkeeper every coin, he had. *"Here my friend, God be with you!"* he said, casting away the small bowl worn from many days of begging for alms. The bowl bounced against a wall, making an empty hollow sound. There was no more need for that.

Going back to his staff it felt different somehow, he would still need it to help navigate back getting used to his new eyesight.

It was hard to concentrate. He reached for a nearby stool steading himself leaning against the walls as he walked. Entering the city, he saw dust from many years of use fall onto his hands something he had only felt before.

He'd close his eyes, to walk normal, but then immediately opened them afraid of losing his eyesight. The colors and shapes of things he'd only imagined now took form. The world was brand new, unrecognizable it was glorious!

This new world was unreal and fascinating. He even felt something on the inside, it felt different, even more bizarre. It was almost too much to handle. He had to get there, slipping and falling along the way determined to see Jesus.

Just ahead he could hear the crowd walking faster, his heart beating at a furious pace. Barely catching his breath. His excitement grew as he saw Jesus surrounded by the people that had come to see Him.

At first it was hard to speak, he began to murmur, *"I can see."* Tears filled his eyes. *"Jesus, JESUS, I can see!"* Immediately people turned around realizing who he was. The crowd parted his voice became louder as between sobs, he said, *"I can see! For the first time in my life I can see!"* The crowd became deathly silent. He threw his staff to the ground, striking the stone walkway the sound echoed throughout the city.

Pressing further into the crowd, he reached out touching the faces of those around him. Hearing their voices as they talked about this miracle. He looked deeply into their eyes, crying and laughing at the same time. He spoke their names: *"Joash, I can see."* His words turned into a deep sob as he wiped the tears away, barely able to talk. *"Bethany, Bethany my child. I can see"* Low and solemn, it was a sound of total amazement and surrender.

Some wondered what sort of magic this was, while others began dancing and praising God. The Jewish priests that had followed him were arguing in the back of the crowd. They looked like little old men, their faces strained with confusion.

Stumbling through the crowd, he rushed towards Jesus. He covered his eyes trying to protect them from the blinding sun. He accidently knocked over a Jewish priest who was headed towards Jesus to complain about some religious law.

He reached down and helped the priest and as they rose the crowd began to laugh praising God even louder. As the priest realized who he was he ran from him, scared and amazed at the same time.

The sky was bright he could barely see. He heard the familiar cackle of the ravens as he watched them circle the sky. He saw their piercing eyes looking down amazed at this unfolding miracle. He stumbled forward, falling at Jesus feet, catching his breath. He lay there, weeping for joy, sobbing and praising God reaching out to the man who had performed this great miracle.

The ravens now curious flew closer. They seemed to be enthralled by everything that was happening. They had been his companions, often sitting in the town square by the pool of Siloam. They sensed something wonderful had happened as they landed among the crowd.

Hardly able to speak, sitting up, he reached out to Jesus. *"I am not worthy! I am not worthy! Jesus, why me?*

Jesus reached down to embrace the newly sighted man and smiled. *"I am my Father's son, come to help all people see. As I walked by you I could feel the enormous love you have for those around you, these people who could be cruel and unloving. But you cared for them overlooking their faults. Go, share with the world the colors that you had only felt, but now can see."*

He put his hands-on Jesus feet, doing the best he could to brush them off, his tears leaving small spots on the dust from His travels. *"I'm not worthy Lord, how could you love someone like me?"*

Jesus lifted him up, *"It's the red, the green, and it's the blue. Few have experienced what you now have seen. Your loving and contrite heart, held no malice or unforgiveness, this is what brought you your sight and healed your soul. You approached me with no need as you listened to the words I preached. In this world, few care about anything but themselves. Blinded by the very world they have created, they are content to sit, standing for nothing, falling for everything and giving very little, while requiring much."*

Jesus continued speaking, *"You've given much and asked for little. You found joy despite your pain, returning love for hate, joy for fear and faith beyond measure. You've seen what few have felt. Show them real freedom. Help those who are truly blind see."*

Jesus held him and spoke to him speaking silently so no one could hear. He then walked away. The once blind man felt a renewed spirit a warm sensation deep in his heart. It was hard to explain. He felt loved from the top of his head to the bottom of his feet. An unrecognizable calmness invaded his life and gave him a new confidence that filled his spirit and nourished his soul. Watching Jesus walk away, he praised God for being able to see the unseen and feel the unfelt. He was free.

The crowd now motivated by what they had witnessed, erupted into a new frantic voice. The requests rang out, *"Jesus what about me?"* They heard but did not listen. They saw but did not see. Blinded by their own needs, they were deaf to the needs of others.

The crowd moved towards Him as some fell. Peter, who was walking behind Jesus, stood his ground and with his strong burly arms lifted those who had fallen. Looking towards the crowd in complete disappointment they grew silent. They respected Peter they knew not to make him angry. Peter could be loving. But if pushed, the fisherman's impatience would come into play and they knew he was a man of physical power.

Jesus walked ahead. His words real and without precedent. To the right was a man who had not walked since birth.

Reaching down to the man He spoke one word, "Rise." To everyone's amazement, the man rose, walking and leaping and praising God. The wonder of it all moved the crowd into an absolute frenzy. Even Peter and the disciples wondered if they could control these folks, desperately looking for answers. The disciples had their hands full. But somehow, they were able to calm the crowd.

They insisted that He look at them, touch them, heal them. The Jewish priest now besides themselves mocked His power as that of the devil's. But the only one listening was the devil himself. The priest could expel everyone present from the temple, but this kept no one from reaching out to Jesus, this prophet in their midst.

Jesus stopped due to the pressing crowd. His disciples, like a powerful wave, parted the crowd to allow Him to take a few more steps. It never bothered Him. His spirit was pure. He never reacted in an impatient or mean manner. He was a man of peace. His presence overcame their fear and any troubling spirit they had. People were covered by His calm, serene presence, overwhelmed by His confident manner.

Jesus was on a mission, reaching out to those that needed Him. He lived only to serve.

He had become a rock star in His own time. As the crowds grew He taught from a boat just to have somewhere to stand. He shared the many fundamental, simple truths that changed their lives.

He performed unnatural fantastic miracles they wondered *"How could any man accomplish this?"* As He walked, many were healed, they listened and learned many amazing truths.

It was His words that eased their greatest need. Broken hearts were made whole they left the past behind holding fast to this new life that Jesus preached.

As He looked towards the heavens and spoke, *"Peace be still!"* even the storms listened to Him. That same power to overcome the storms stilled the thunder and lightning in the lives of the people who believed.

Walking through the crowds, His disciples noticed that He was tiring. They looked for a place where He could rest. Peter noticed it first. He saw a small space near the path they were walking on.

He took the lead pushing back the crowd giving Jesus room. Peter could be loud and annoying, but when he spoke people listened.

His deep, gravelly voice could be heard above all the confusion. *"Move aside, give us room!"* People began moving opening a path for Jesus. Peter's brawn was sometimes more powerful than his brain.

The other disciples followed Peter's lead. They moved a donkey that was tied up near a bench that was determined to stay close to Jesus, a few chickens who had found some shade flew away, protesting loudly. A few ravens that had followed the action found a new place to sit. Soon the small, dusty area became a place where Jesus could rest. Sitting on a make-shift bench constructed of old olive oil barrels and planks of rough wood. Just beside the donkey a local Samaritan woman approached bringing Him water. Jesus smiled and blessed her as she walked away.

Jesus was exhausted, no matter how great the mission, peoples unrelenting needs could wear you down. His disciples began setting up a perimeter. The crowd could not get enough of Him, they sat and waited, no one was going anywhere.

Suddenly without warning close to Peter's side, a small disturbance broke out as several women pushed their children towards Jesus. When they broke through, Peter yelled, *"Get your kids away!"*

Before he could get to them, the children snuck through Matthew's legs, almost tripping him. Peter, watching the event tried to hold back his laughter. But he did no better, when a child accidently tripped him, and he fell face first onto the dusty road. Now everyone was laughing.

He rose, his face beet red perturbed by the kids actions he brushing off his clothes. He turned towards the crowd as the disciples became silent, trying hard not to laugh. Peter began to launch out at the crowd when the laughter of the children caught his attention, echoing off the local stone houses.

Smiling at the children's exploits, Jesus began laughing as He watched Peter finish dusting off his clothes. Before Peter could yell out again, Jesus raised His hand and said, *"Let the children come to me, my old friend."* As the children got close to Him, He reached out and held each child, hugging them, His eyes full of love and compassion.

Peter was indignant, his face now a pale red, he looked around quickly making sure no other breach was happening. Jesus turned looking at Peter, *"My brother Peter, if you want to enter the Kingdom of God you must become like these little children."* There was silence Peter was confused. But his confusion turned to a peaceful expression when he sensed the calm spirit that the children brought to Jesus. He wondered what Jesus meant. *"Jesus was so tired ministering for days, why these children?"* he thought. *"How do I become a kid again?"*

It was evident that Jesus was becoming empowered by the children's presence. They believed anything was possible and their belief was unshakeable. Jesus was not ministering to them. In fact, the children with their unwavering spirits, undeniable faith and hearts full of love were ministering to Him. Their only need was to be near Him.

Each hug from a child lifted His spirits increasing His strength, being near their beautiful hearts.

They connected with Him on a spiritual level that few knew then or even know today. They had no hidden agenda their hearts were pure, their faith strong, their gifts intact. Jesus laughed and smiled enjoying every moment. The crowd noticed every move of the children. As they watched this incredible moment they laughed while others wiped away tears.

Not one child asked for anything for themselves. They were there to share their love with Him. Dancing and singing without regard of anyone, they expressed their love, overjoyed by the event. They were there to give. They ministered to Him and were there to serve Him.

A child asked Jesus if He could help his sister hear. She had been deaf her whole life, Jesus reached down smiled and held her, the crowd listening intently. He touched her ears and as he did there was a moment of complete silence. She turned to be near her brother and as she did she heard the ravens for the very first time. She began to giggle, to cry and dance, free as a bird. The ravens seemed to join in as they started bobbing up and down on their perches.

The silence was broken the crowd started singing praises to God. First softly but as they sang each line they became louder and stronger everyone was affected by this spirit of love and joy. There was not a dry eye in the place. Except for the priest who had nothing to say they stood befuddled by all that had just happened.

Running towards her mother the little boy's sisters face was all aglow with this new gift she had been given. The people witnessing the event realized that something deep within them started to change. They began to understand the power of Jesus's words. They were no longer as blind or deaf as they had been. The miracles they now witnessed changed them as they watched their children singing and dancing.

This moment created a new spirit in them forever. They began to enter the doorway to the Kingdom of God for the very first time.

There is no higher calling than that of a servant. It's a servant's heart that brings people to a place where healing begins. Jesus was and is the greatest example of the power of giving. His ministry focused on the needs of others. As a true servant He changed the world we live in. And He stands beside His Father saying, "Come and dance."

Everywhere we turn today. People ask, "*What's in it for me?*" We have become a selfish nation, calling out the name of Jesus, imploring Him to do something for us.

We're so self-involved we rarely see the needs of others blind to what is right in front of us. There is a power drawn from the Kingdom of God that is so fantastic that it can change nations even our whole world. When we pray for others and give to those in need, pray for their healing, their lives, you are activating a true power that brings the healing and help you need. You gain the amazing power to live an uncompromising, fantastic existence, secure under your Father's wing.

Jesus teaching's centered around the fact that you should not worry about the clothes you wear or the food you need. He knows when you reach out to help others see, then that hidden path you've been looking for suddenly opens before you. When you help someone heal, your healing comes with it. As you help others to find their answers the ones you seek will come. In fact, it's our preoccupation with ourselves that keeps us from receiving the real power we need in our lives.

The Bible says:

Consider the ravens: for they neither sow nor reap; which neither have storehouse nor barn; and God feedeth them: how much more are ye better than the fowls?

Luke 12:24

But this I say, He which soweth sparingly shall reap also sparingly; and he which soweth bountifully shall reap also bountifully.

2 Corinthians 9:6

Be not deceived; God is not mocked: for whatsoever a man soweth, that shall he also reap.

Galatians 6:7

And let us not be weary in well doing: for in due season we shall reap if we faint not.

Galatians 6:9

Jesus is saying to give and not take He understands by doing so you unleash a powerful weapon that nothing on earth can stop, called love.

Jesus your prime example of how to live was a servant. His mission was to give. He gave it all even His life for you. His power of love, His ministry was so mighty that it affects billions today. His power to heal was activated because He was in tune with His spirit. His only need, His only calling was to serve. Humble and contrite, Jesus was a powerhouse of love and spiritual action His motivation was not selfish, but about serving others. Once your spirit connects with God's heart, miracles happen. If you can't move the mountain in front of you it's probably because you you only see the mountain you see.

Jesus said:

Verily, verily, I say unto you, He that believeth on me, the works that I do shall he do also; and greater works than these shall he do; because I go unto my Father.

John 14:12

Greater love hath no man than this, that a man lay down his life for his friends.

John 15:13

Jesus did not say you will enter the Kingdom of Heaven; He said that if you want to enter the Kingdom of God, you must be as these little children.

And when he was demanded of the Pharisees, when the kingdom of God should come, he answered them and said, the kingdom of God cometh not with observation: Neither shall they say, Lo here! or, lo there! for, behold, the kingdom of God is within you.

Luke 17:20-21

As you comprehend the Kingdom of God is within "YOU," Then nothing, and nobody, nowhere, at no time and in no way, in any place, province, city or country, had better get in your way.

You have the *"**KINGDOM OF GOD WITHIN YOU**"* In case you didn't get that "YOU HAVE THE KINGDOM OF GOD WITHIN YOU" The devil will make you believe that you have no authority in this world, pointing out your weaknesses and convincing you that you're without help. He fears the day that you realize that THE POWER OF GOD, the almighty, miracle generating, mountain moving, King of all Kings is within you.

Then he called his twelve disciples together, and gave them power and authority over all devils, and to cure diseases.

Luke 9:1

One of the greatest deceptions that satan has put in the church is that healing and miracles are not for today. Jesus said "*Verily, verily, I say unto you, He that believeth on me, the works that I do shall he do also; and greater works than these shall he do.*" Satan wants a powerless comfortable church, he loves you attending there, he will do everything in his power to keep you from gaining or maintaining power.

Once you realize you have this new power your world will be changed overnight.

Becoming a kid again comes from realizing that you are now taking the power of satan away from him. He's concerned that once you realize the truth he will lose everything. What would happen in your world if you engaged this power of love, prayed only for the needs of others and lived with a servant's heart. As you reached out to the world and people became healed by the hundred's, lives changed by the thousands, how many hits on "You Tube" do you think you'd get.

When your spirit comes alive, hell runs for cover. They're afraid that you will realize what just happened. The power of the almighty, all consuming, all powerful, God without end the Lord of the Universe, the mighty King of our world, the creator of all things is now residing in "YOU." All the gifts with their power and brilliance are now available to you. As you ask God to come into your life you become a brand-new creation. Nothing in hell can stop a believer who understands this compelling truth.

*Therefore, if any man be in Christ, <u>he is a new creature</u>: **old things are passed away**; behold, **all things are become new.***

2 Corinthians 5:17

Not somethings, or anything but everything. All things have become new. Believe it, accept it, receive it.

The more you yield to this new spirit led life the more valuable it becomes. Without it you travel a path leading to an unwinnable consequence. All the pain you've felt, the wars you've fought have been in a physical world ruled by satan. Your old self has tried to fight your way out of a bag with no opening. You've done the best you could fighting the devil without God. But It's been like trying to fight an armored Bradley tank with a pea shooter.

We don't have the weapons necessary to fight this spiritual battle. It's the devil's playground, without spiritual wisdom and understanding, without the Kingdom of God, the devil will win. He made the rules that corrupt, kill and steal in this world. If he doesn't like the way it's going, he can change the rules to fit his desires. He has only one loyalty, and that's to himself.

You're a spiritual person in a physical body. That spiritual part of you is dead until it joins with the Kingdom of God. Children understand they've been given an uncompromising love and faith. As adults we stumble and fight our way through the darkness blinded by our everyday conquests. We hand over the gifts given as children. Children are given gifts for protection until they are old enough to decide which road they will take. Chose the wrong road and it can destroy your hopes, dreams and any belief in the future.

When you enter the Kingdom of God, you become an exclusive member of a very powerful club. Suddenly you increase the amount of potential brain and spiritual power you possess.

This power is a gateway to becoming a spiritual super hero. Living on a new physical, spiritual and mental level. You begin to understand life on a whole new level.

As you implement this new life your renewed spirit invades your broken heart and heals any lost dreams or hopes you may have had. The revelation of God's love will help any blind person see. You may be blinded by the brightness of the light for a moment. But then you will see the world in a whole new way. The colors will become vibrant, you'll feel red to the bottom of your soul.

There is only one cure for a broken heart. You need to become a member of God's family. Your vision will change as you begin this new adventure. You begin to see the world as a child sees the world, full of promise and mystery. You will feel the need to climb a few trees or run like the wind. Color a tree burnt amber with your Crayola Crayons just because you see it that way.

You can soar like you never thought possible. You'll comprehend the light and figure out what's wrong or right. You begin to live as you learn to give. Your heart turns into a cure for those who are insecure. Learning what it really means to play. Your free on every new day.

YOUR 3ᴿᴰ SECRET MISSION

1. You've learned that you need an **unshakeable plan**. No matter what comes at you. Like Old Blue we follow the clues, until we reach the good news.

2. Understanding that your parents, friends and coworkers are not your enemy. **Your enemy is satan** who has planned to take you out. Don't give him a toehold or foothold in your life. Because it will soon become a stronghold. He will steal and kill your dreams, hopes and any peace you have.

3. In this spiritual warfare you can see clearly all the beauty of this world if you follow what is written. Miracles will happen, sight will be restored. When you enter the Kingdom of God you now become something else for satan to contend with. And the heart of a servant changes your life and the life of others. **Becoming a kid again is finding your way to a brighter day. Defeating the traps satan has laid, by holding on to the promises God has made**.

<u>**REDVERB:**</u> Learning about giving is the path to living.

As a child if you were raised in a Godly home, in a loving environment, with parents that had a giving spirit you could become a beacon of hope and faith. Since it would be easier to maintain the gifts given to you as a child. But if you were raised in the middle of a thunderstorm, full of lighting and hell then you may have lost those amazing gifts you were given as a kid. You learned to survive but at a great cost. This mission includes asking God to reveal to you the mighty weapons of spiritual warfare. By first asking God to let you enter His Kingdom and receive a new heart, a new faith and the weapons needed to win the war.

It's impossible to become a kid again without these tools. You'll need them in future secret missions.

It is hard to lay aside the problems of this life while you're try to overcome a challenging past. The secret is to decide to live in the present and not focus on the past. When you believe in a positive future with God as your co-pilot you create a peaceful existence where joy is resident.

You'll always have challenges, disappointments maybe you've lost someone you love or lost love all together. The difference is you now have God's word to teach you, His love to reach you. The power and understanding you receive is limitless.

Laying the past aside you no longer strive but thrive. When you begin to live again, you'll find a way to give again. You'll not wonder you'll know which path to take and which way to go.

Drugs, alcohol, hatred, depression and fear are gateways to a scary and bumpy road. Leading to nowhere, promising nothing, awarding heartache and pain as its ultimate gift. That's a gift you will never have to unwrap if you travel down God's highway.

You're not perfect, none of us are. God greets us in our imperfection, with mercy, grace and forgiveness. It's the stepping stone enabling you to complete your mission. Most folks would give everything to experience the peace and joy that God gives. And it's free. Just reach out and accept it. God's love will overtake you, remake you.

It's the secret that enables healing to begin. No longer defeated by this world, you gain brand new super powers as a new citizen in the Kingdom of God. It's the first step you need to take to become a kid again.

REDVERB: Don't fear death, fear not living

Failure is simply the opportunity to begin again, this time more intelligently.

Henry Ford

There are some things one can only achieve by a deliberate leap in the opposite direction.

Franz Kafka

Take the first step in faith. You don't have to see the whole staircase, just take the first step.

Martin Luther King

A journey of a thousand miles begins with a single step.

Lao Tzu

Do what you can, with what you have, where you are.

Theodore Roosevelt

Start by doing what's necessary: then do what's possible: and suddenly you're doing the impossible.

St Francis Of Assisi

Moment of Mirth:

A minister died and found himself waiting in line to be judged and admitted to heaven. While waiting, he started a conversation with the man in front of him. The pastor asked what he did while on earth. *"I was a taxi driver from Noo Yawk City,"* the fellow replied. Suddenly the angel guarding the gate called out, *"Next!"* and the New York taxi driver stepped up. Trumpets began to blare and a whole parade of angels came to the taxi driver's side putting a gold crown on his head and seating him in a solid gold chariot filled with diamonds and all kind of jewels. Magnificent, beautiful horses pulled the chariot and as he proceeded through the gates the chief angel handed him a solid gold staff loading his chariot with rare fruits and cheeses.

He then gave him the keys to the most beautiful mansion on a hill overlooking heaven. The pastor seeing all of this could not wait to see his gifts. *"Next!"* the angel said. The pastor rose and went forward the angel handed the minister a used wooden staff and some bread and water. He then handed him a key to a small rusty shack at the low end of heaven. No angels, no parade. The minister was perplexed, he asked the angel, *"That guy who just went in was a taxi driver, you gave him a golden staff, a parade and the most beautiful home in heaven! I spent my entire life as a minister and get nothing! How can that be?"*

The angel replied, *"In heaven it's all about the results. All your people slept through your sermons. But while riding in his taxi thousands of people dedicated their lives to God making promises to go to church if they would live till their next stop; and thousands more prayed for the very first time!"*

And, behold, I come quickly; and my reward is with me, to give every man according as his work shall be. I am Alpha and Omega, the beginning and the end, the first and the last.

Revelation 22:12-13

TASK #3: Buy a paddleball the one with the rubber string. Keep playing until you reach one hundred without missing or stopping.

CHAPTER

4

what Baggage?

I love Lucky Charms. There's something about them that keeps me tied to being a kid. Those tiny little Leprechauns making green clovers and yellow diamond-shaped marshmallows. Nothing tasted as good or magical. You picked up a purple horseshoe made a wish and knew it would come true.

As a kid, I had no clue that God existed. But I did believe in Leprechauns and the Keebler elves. They made those tasty cookies in oak trees as they danced, singing the night away. Always protecting their pot of gold. Because every time they turned around, someone was eating their cookies or trying to steal their Lucky Charms.

Each day was a new beginning starting an exciting, incredible adventure. There was always something new to do and see.

We found great ways to play. The world was full of amazing, undiscovered places. Rocks became castles, trees were begging to be climbed and a little mud make great hand grenades. Your friends remembered the day you jumped on a live mud grenade to save them, you were their hero.

There were Saturday morning cartoons with their fantastic, powerful characters. You felt the world would be safe if Superman could stay away from Kryptonite and Batman had Robin. But Leprechauns made more sense they had that pot of gold. It had to be out there somewhere.

When we saw a rainbow, we'd get on our bikes and chase it down. Peddling as fast as we could to get to that magical place at the bottom of the rainbow. Where the Leprechauns stored all their gold. We were poor and could only imagine how many Lucky Charms that gold would buy.

Growing up you may have given all your magic away without thinking. Encountering life, you saw it through different eyes. You went from Saturday morning cartoons and those dancing elves on oak street to a new reality on Wall Street. The world became a different place.

You began to see things as they were and not how they could be. Reality replaced imagination. It didn't happen overnight, it wasn't long till the Leprechauns and elves quit dancing. No more pirates to chase, no rafts to sail around the world or rocket ships to Mars. And then you were stuck in eight a.m. traffic with five miles to go, hoping to get there by nine.

As children, we were impervious to pain, able to stop speeding bullets running faster than a locomotive and leaping buildings with a single bound. My mom got mad the day she found me using her favorite red towel to fly like Superman. Or when I brought home a cardboard box which was my new spaceship launching it in the front yard. I reached faraway planets, far away from the pain.

Sometimes your only hope is that there's enough coffee left to get you through the day. *"Okay, who used all the cream? Has anyone seen the Sweet and Low? Okay, where's Ralph?!!"*

There was a time when life was simple and uncomplicated stars were bright and mysterious. Cats loved chasing strings and the man in the moon was real. Then someone said that it's impossible to fly, and rafts would sink. And you believed them. Which ended your voyage to Atlantis and threw cold water on ever reaching Bora-Bora. That Superman cape just became a red towel and your spaceship became an old refrigerator box. You threw out the box and gave back the towel to your mom. Somehow, it lost all its power.

Clouds became just clouds so you gave up looking up. Lucky Charms was replaced with the newest breakfast cereal made with healthy non-fat, no calorie, organic, gluten-free ingredients.

A cereal pressed together with virgin olive oil topped with an artificial sweetener, a cereal made with vegan twigs and nuts from South America. It was brought here on donkey backs over the Andes and guaranteed to extend our lives. Full of anti-oxidants but tasted like the paper this book is written on. *"So much healthier than Lucky Charms!"* But no fun at all. Made to extend our lives.

But what kind of life have you extended when you wake up feeling down. You try to rise, grasping for support, hoping to carry on. You go back to bed, lay there thinking about the day, going over the data, looking for answers online. The next morning life's complications stole your dreams and made it impossible to sleep.

There are apps for cats and cowboy hats. Big league scores and elephant tracks, mac attacks and amazing facts. But not one app showing you how to get back, what you lack.

Do you remember climbing trees as a kid? You could see for miles, the birds singing, the sky blue, it was incredible to feel the wind as it ran through the leaves on the trees. Now there's an app for that. You keep searching for answers to life's many problems but it's hard to type into Google the right questions when you don't know what to ask.

The wonderment of how caterpillars become butterflies and how cats can jump that high turned into a discussion about stocks and bonds and how they can go so low. Wall Street took over Oak Street where we used to play *"Red Rover, Red Rover come on over."* But no one is playing, no one is coming, no matter how loud you yell.

It can be a world of tension and stress with the reality that weeds are hard to kill. Some of the things we've picked up as adults seem to be insurmountable we've tried to adjust, change, even move a little faster.

Your world becomes more confusing as you've tried to understand how people can be so cruel, unforgiving and uncaring. At times lost not knowing where to turn.

You rumble on to your late appointments, in an empty car, with a mistaken identity. Lost as a Route 66 gas station, living a planned life, making turns where there are no roads. Driving and drinking your Gingerbread latte with a twist of orange peel and light foam. You tweet your thoughts while your GPS looks for a new route to work. And when you get there, somehow, your still lost.

You gaze at the map you so carefully laid out, asking yourself *"Where am I, and am I there yet?"*

Life takes its toll. You may have been disregarded even mistreated mentally and physically. Which created a troubling pain in your chest when a tiny crack began to form.

At first barely noticeable, more irritating than painful. But something had to be done with this new development. Of course, you never wanted anyone to see your pain. The only safe answer was to pack it away.

So, you found an old suitcase your father had and dusted it off, checked the locks making sure they worked. It felt comfortable to hold onto and reasonable to carry. It was a burden, but it was hardly noticeable if it stayed locked and packed away.

This was your first step into adulthood, packing away your emotional baggage, putting it in a safe place where no one could see it. Out of sight out of mind, right?

As time marched on you became more proficient at packing away any new hurts or pains. It was easier to pack them away than understand them. But it wasn't long till that small suitcase was filled with broken dreams, unforgiveness and bitterness. It became harder to shut. You eventually got it to close without showing any pain. It was heavy, so you leaned a little to the left as you walked and smiled to the right doing your best to balance things out.

You rush through life, hating Mondays. You can't wait for the weekend. As you get older the weeks fly by till months seem like weeks and years like months. As kids we talked about our ages in fractions *"I'm five and a half"* as if that made us seem older. Then we couldn't wait to be sixteen, so we could drive, then twenty-one because we could finally be an adult with all its privileges. Some of us were even excited about becoming fifty-five because we got discounts on strawberry pancakes at IHOP.

Life moves fast. It becomes more difficult to pack your suitcase as more things pile up. It wasn't long till you wondered what happened to your life. Your bike now dusty with flat tires as you have given up looking for that pot of gold.

Your belief system can change. If you listen to the adverse influences around you. It can turn faith into failure. And peace may just become a word spoken when you order pie. It's important to live in the real world and not make waves. A fact is a fact, right?

You may no longer see the world through a kid's eyes. Light can eventually become darkness and love hard to find. Hope may end up in right field waiting for a ball to come its way. Reality sets in and the glass is half empty. It can be hard to ever imagine it being half full again.

You may have fought to stay in the light, challenging the darkness, believing that better days were ahead. It took all your strength to hold on to your gifts, your weapons and childhood dreams. Even so be careful that during those struggles you didn't pack an overnight bag.

Others wounded you with cruel words that might have been unintentional, but still hurt, the damage done. Folks frustrated by their station in life may say words that have no meaning. Or they may have spoken with the intention to hurt which can result in a broken spirit far more difficult to heal than a broken bone. Words that hurt spoken and unspoken can rob you of life causing a deep wound that's hard to cure.

Remember folks who point fingers at anyone standing near them never realize that as one finger points forward, three-point back. The reason that people blame others for their problems is because they themselves are the real problem. Their only choice is to fix themselves or blame others for their short comings. So much easier to blame.

Unfortunately, there may have been times when you caused pain to others. These are the hardest things to unpack. Being honest with your self is the key to finding your way. Hopefully, life has taught you well and you've grown to the point that you realize what the power of words can do to others.

Navigating through life there are some who take joy in hurting others. Trying in desperation to bring others into the same world of pain they live in. They may be ensconced in jealousy, greed even hatred and this can affect anyone. If you're not careful you could retaliate by grabbing tools from the devil's toolbox designed to steal joy from others but you as well.

Every moment you live, every tick of the clock you make decisions to bring forth life or death, pain or peace, faith or failure.

Becoming a kid again gets you back to a place where life was fun, when the pain wasn't there. When the only thing that mattered was reading the map that led to Blackbeard's treasure, and laughing for no reason.

It's time to bring the light to the burdens that you've carried and hand them over to God. He'll teach you how to run and have fun, instead of living life where you freak, because things are so bleak.

Is it possible to unpack the past when your suitcases have become so heavy? When your heart has become weighed down by everyday events. Walking around with a heavy heart of stone. You may not even realize how much luggage you're carrying. Denying the problem doesn't make it go away. But it's difficult to walk when you keep packing away the pain.

"Don't worry!" you say I can handle it. Trying to be perfect, without blemish, because it's more important to act like everything's okay, than being okay.

Standing there in your perfection someone comes along and steals your joy, trying to steal back the joy they lost. It's amazing that we let others steal our joy, we let others determine if we're going to have a good day or not. Never, ever let anyone at any time steal your joy, the devil knows where your strength lies.

You could have found ways to get by when things got tough. You've learned to hide what matters. Laughing, drinking and drugging your way through life. Let's not deal with the problems, because you can't feel anything, anyway, so who cares. But remember one problem never goes away by creating another. Then one day you open the suitcase trying to remember what the world had done to you. Once it's open whoever is near you gets the full treatment. You wanted them to know how difficult it was to open. It's easy to blame others for making you look inside.

It's time to take inventory, to see the things you stored and packed away. It's time to unpack the past and release those things destined to rob you of your future.

REDVERB: You're the only one that remembers your past or can create a better future. Eliminate the past, celebrate the future.

When you do a small miracle takes place as a tiny area of your heart starts to become flesh again. You gain some room. It's time to fill this area with rediscovered love, patience, faith and joy. Don't be alarmed if you find yourself starting to sing, cry or even laugh. It's been a while since this part of your heart functioned. You feel the need to dance. Warmth begins to fill your heart as the stone begins to fall away. Your spirit becomes renewed and you have an immediate craving for a big bowl of Lucky Charms. Go ahead-they're magical.

God says:

"I will sprinkle clean water on you, and you will be clean; I will cleanse you from all impurities and from your idols. I will give you a new heart and put a new spirit in you; I will remove from you your heart of stone and give you a heart of flesh.

Ezekiel 36: 25-26

How heavy is your heart?

Beware, as you start this new life satan will do everything he can to stop you from going forward. He could inspire someone to kick your newly healed broken heart and it becomes more fragmented. Don't give up, don't give out and whatever you do, don't give in. You don't want to start packing your suitcase again, adding new items. Like pain, impatience, and worry which is the worst of life. If you do, remember to smile because your good at that.

This new joy you felt, no matter how brief, the faith you started to have in the impossible and the hope you possessed will be moved to pack away these new bad items you feel you need. The devil makes It easy to add baggage because suitcases aren't that expensive to buy. Don't you let him once you start a good thing, finish a good thing.

REDVERB: Accept what is, let go of what was, and have faith in what will be. You can't reach out for what's ahead if you hold onto what's behind.

If you don't the shield will drop, protecting you from ever being hurt again. You put up a barrier keeping others out or to keep your feelings in. No one will ever hurt you again. Impervious to pain, you try hard not to feel anything, the skates are off, leaving childhood behind. Survival is all that matters. You solider on, keeping the shield intact because it's safe there.

Faith becomes fear, joy becomes desperation, and any peace that you have is eliminated by depression. You buy a lotto ticket having a little hope, but it's soon gone. It's funny that we think money is the answer. We think about it, pray for it and beg for it, like somehow it can solve everything.

In fact, money can't eliminate the pains you feel. It can't fix a broken heart. It allows you to buy more suitcases to hide even more. They would be beautiful and strong and anyone that saw them would believe you finally made it.

REDVERB: The greatest things in life are not things.

Packing a suitcase is easy when your butler is satan. He's more than willing to help you pack and hide from the truth. He'll load you down with burdens that multiply confusion and divide your strength. You'll soon find yourself hanging out on the corner of Depression Avenue and Give-it-Up lane. If he has his way, he'll bury you under the strife of life, so you'll end up on the End-It-All freeway. *Why suffer anymore?*

A broken heart complicates everything, and the prognosis is not good no matter what the EKG says. Your only hope is to rediscover the gifts and secrets that children possess. How to smile on a cloudy day or dance in the rain. Once you discover these gifts it's time to bring them back into your life.

There's light in the darkness that eliminates the shadows that ruled you. As things become clearer you'll realize just how many suitcases you own. This new reality will shine back into the past and light your way to the future. You'll begin to see clearly how to unpack the pain you've held onto and any unforgiveness you've harbored.

Fantastic things will happen when you lose that tight grip. The past will fall away. That heavy luggage you carried will start to lighten. Relieving your tired shoulders and aching back. Life becomes simple again.

You'll start laughing for no reason and cry for joy. You see the turtles, and horses that float by in the clouds. And feel the overwhelming power of joy that waits for you on the road ahead.

Your heavy heart starts to heal, your vision becomes clear, as you loosen your grip on the past. You begin to see the world as a child sees the world, leaving stress, worry and pain behind. Resentment and suffering no longer have a hold on you.

No bitterness from a long-ago event. Your heart starts to work as planned, your joy expands. People may stare but you won't care as you tear away that shield that surrounded your heart.

The world is full of wonder, each day a new beginning. One more day to love, laugh and climb a tree. To feel the wind softly play hide and seek with your face. Something basic and fundamental rises within your heart, soul and spirit. No more stumbling as you walk, you find yourself skipping a bit. Your heart no longer carries the heavy burdens you bore.

REDVERB: Yesterday is a distant shore, you don't live there anymore. You've opened a door to find a new life forever more.

Find a mud puddle to play in, watch the sun fill in the spaces in the trees where the breezes had been. No regrets about yesterday. The stupid things you did were stupid. The brilliant things stand on their own accord.

Your put on this earth to learn by making mistakes because that's the only way you'll learn. If your making mistakes its because you are challenging life, you're learning new spiritual ninja moves. But remember to learn from them and make them only once.

The power in life, the patience, the love, the overwhelming joy comes from learning to let go and let God. Give Him each day that you live. This journey you're on leads to a place you haven't seen since the first grade.

Leaving burdens behind giving God each day, you'll be consumed by His love and patience. But He can do nothing unless you seek it and allow it. The devil who made plans to take you down now runs from your presence when you decide to unpack the past. His confusion on what to do next overwhelms him. And what is he going to do with all those suitcases your leaving behind? I'm sure he'll find someone to give them to.

When you carried all that weight, you said, *"I don't have a problem!"* as your back ached. In some cases, the past could have become so engrained in your life that you could see no way to let go of the handle.

Life is what you make it. If it's your choice to continue carrying the weight, there's nothing anyone can do to help. You can hear the truth, but no one has the power to make you accept the truth. Only you have that power.

God himself doesn't have the power to change you. You and only you have that power. As sad as it sounds you can become comfortable, familiar living with pain. Afraid of change.

You may have heard folks exclaim," *I'm going to take this to my grave."* The good news is by holding on to depressive memories and negative vibes, and unforgiveness you will experience a shorter life span. That way you won't have so long to carry your luggage.

If change scares you, here's something new, developed through years of research by the brightest minds in the industry. It's a small pill just discovered called LGF, the good news it has no terrible side effects like blindness, kidney shut down, restless leg syndrome or anal leakage, thank God!

LGF was created and developed in secret Swedish labs with over fifty-five years of intensive scientific research. Made with the greatest natural ingredients available. Guaranteed to create a brand new you.

ONE LEGAL NOTE:

It does not help overactive bladders or the heartache of psoriasis nor does it work overnight like Ex-Lax. Ex-Lax working overnight never sounded like a good idea anyway.

LGF is pure and straightforward. Once taken you're going to feel a euphoria that you've never felt before. There is an internal change in your outlook on life. The world will be a new positive, powerful place. You'll notice the sky is blue.

You'll see the world differently, you'll laugh more often, and sleep like a bear hibernating for winter. You'll dream amazing dreams. The effects are fantastic.

Caution: Don't take LGF unsupervised, because of the effect of this pill. Don't operate heavy machinery under its influence. Prepare for an out of body experience so wear warm clothes.

LGF will cause a massive release of the recent past. It will wipe out the bad memories and amplify the good ones.

LGF changes your perspective on life emotionally, and you'll feel better physically. Your steps will be lighter, you no longer carry the weight of the world on your shoulders. People who maintain a positive outlook on life live healthier, longer lives.

There is only one catch you must take it.

When you do, get ready, life changes drastically. Through the magic of modern medicine, you'll feel as light as a canary that inhaled helium.

You'll stand more upright. You learn to walk again without a limp from carrying life's burdens for, so long. Hope will arise, joy will greet you every morning and you'll discover the heart of a child, filled with peace, faith and the ability to love again.

The **Let Go Forever** (LGF) pilot program is highly recommended for those who believe they don't have a problem. Or just don't want to admit they do. The truth is simple but profound. **If you don't change your life, then nothing in your life will change.**

When you join the "Let Go Forever" pilot program, the past falls by the wayside. You'll have an immediate desire to play. Step two in the program, call your friends get a slip and slide, lots of chocolate milk, some brownies and have fun in the sun. Be aware it will become natural to smile, even experience an over dose of laughter.

Now that you have got to this place, it's time to change the road you've been on. If your days were full of negative, depressing, joy-killing, love-denying, hurt-causing, painful moments, then it's time to let go of those things that held you captive. Which allows you to enjoy the freedom of a renewed heart and open mind.

Moments occur when seconds pass then minutes happen. Never let a second go by in your life without a solemn, beautiful peace. The kind that comes from concentrating on fun instead of the thinking of negative things when the day is done.

There are certain words in the English language that are small and powerful. Like the word "*do,*" you need to "*do*" something different if you want things to change. If you "*do*" different things, then you will make different things happen.

Another great small in stature word that is big and powerful is the word "*If.*" "*If*" only you would have, "*If*" only you could have because you knew you should have. "*If*" only you were smarter or taller maybe better looking or had money, then you could have done something. The initial step in creating who you want to be, is to accept who and what you are. Because life is not about finding yourself. ***It's about creating yourself.***

These two massive words will change your life or stop you from being a greater version of yourself. It's your decision. Life drastically changes "If" you "do" something to change it. It's your choice. This daily decision will free you like a bird out of its cage or imprison you like a thief. It's your choice.

It's time to be free, let it go, find a way "*Don't try, do!*" When you "*Do*" you will receive gifts that will astonish you. Holding on to the past keeps your hands full. God cannot give you anything new unless you empty your hands of the things you carried. If your hands are full of the past, there's no room for the future. Let go and enable God to show, you the gifts and knowledge He has in store for you. Here's the answer "*Let Go Forever!*"

"*If*" can be a miracle inducing positive beginning of a brand-new day for you. "*If only you would try, you will soon find out why!*" this step is so important to you. I challenge you to "*do*" something for you, to take a chance. I know "*If*" you "*do,*" you will never be the same.

"*Come to me, all you who are **weary and burdened**, and I will give you **rest**. Take my yoke upon you and "**LEARN" from me**, for I am gentle and humble in heart, and you will find "REST" for your souls. For my yoke is easy and my burden is light.*"

Matthew 11:28

Jesus is saying, "Put your suitcase down, come and follow me."

"Are you ready?" It can be scary but when the shield goes down but you'll feel the warmth of the sunrise once again. The clear, cool breeze will calm you and send away all those items that you had packed away, that kept you from becoming all you can be.

It's your turn to dream, to care and to forgive. Letting go of the weight that so easily beset you. Peace will overtake you, as you start this new journey of being a kid again. Rekindling joy, having hope, embracing peace.

Your broken heart will be healed.

REDVERB: Risk is a component of change and change is the main ingredient of growth. The speed of growth is always determined by the amount of risk you're willing to take.

Today is fun, tomorrow is great, my life is changing, and I can't wait…

A life not lived says I could have, I should have. I would have.

Red Devine

YOUR 4ᵀᴴ SECRET MISSION

1. Have an unshakeable plan

2. Fight for the right to stay in the light

3. Don't be blinded by this world the kingdom of God is within you

4. Imagination creates reality

5. Decide to change and "do" it

As always, should you or any of your Christian force be caught or compromised, the Secretary will disavow any knowledge of your actions. This message will self-destruct if five seconds! God Speed...

Any mission accomplished, though it may seem impossible, has at its core a problem to be solved or an error that needs to be corrected. Your mission, if you decide to accept it, is to find the child within and by doing so relearn the secrets that all children possess. Reclaim that which you've lost, renew that which has been stolen and bring back to life the hopes you lost and abandoned. This is the gateway to living in a constant state of joy and peace shored up by a love that never ends.

The "Christian Impossible" leader's instructions are as follows:

"With men, this is impossible, but with God all things are possible"

Matthew 19:26

Let go of the past, embrace hope, live only for the day. You can't carry on if you have too much to carry out. Release it, let it go; There is only one person that regret, unforgiveness, bitterness and holding a grudge affects, and that's you.

God cannot give you anything unless you give Him everything. It's when you surrender that you don't hinder what God has planned for you. It becomes fun to be alive. Let God give you back what you gave away. Jesus came to this world to save that which was lost. *"What have you lost?"*

He will help you find it again. Let go of those who hurt you, used you, abused and bruised you.

Create a brand-new you, walking in cool new shoes, getting rid of those old-time blues.

If you harbor the past, you lose your future. And you'll never have the tools to deal with the present. You're right. It was wrong what they did. As hard as it seems you must wonder what made them the way they are. In most cases the abuser was abused and used. That frustration drives them. There is no excuse for their actions but understanding that fact will help you answer that most important question you have asked. *"Why?"*

It's hard to lift your spirits when your burden is so heavy. By releasing the bitterness, unforgiveness and even a deep hatred you open your heart to receive unconditional love. Unpack the pain and you will gain the ability to fly leaving every weight behind. Freedom always comes from being free.

It's time to dance in the rain!

It may seem impossible to unlock that suitcase since it has been locked for so long but give God a chance. He will provide the key to open the lock and throw away the burdens you've carried.

*"**Let us lay aside every weight**, and the sin that so easily besets us, and let us run with patience the race that is set before us."*

Hebrews 12:1

*"For everyone that **A**sketh receiveth; and he that **S**eeketh findeth; and to him that **K**nocketh; it shall be opened.*

Luke 11:10

Look at the first letter of each action stated it spells the word **A.S.K.** that's the starting point! If you ask-seek-knock you will open any jammed-up area in your life.

You need to ask to receive, seek till you find and knock until the door opens wide. Once opened seek the knowledge to keep it open. Find a good local church that preaches Gods word. Full of great people willing to share and help you continue to find the answers you're looking for. The Bible is full of advice and wisdom that has survived thousands of years **tap into its power**. Putting a good plan into place is a major step to renewing your faith in the impossible and improbable things we call life. It will bring you back to the simple life of being a kid. Give Him everything. Investigate that closet where you put that last suitcase you owned. There in the back of the closet in the dark. You locked this one up good then locked the door and threw away the key. You put duct tape around it wrapped it with chains and hid it under some old blankets. It may have been some horrible event or tragedy that hurts deeply. It seems impossible to forgive, improbable to forget.

This stole your joy in the first place. A complete release will bring amazing peace. It may not happen overnight or a week or month. But as you begin to let go your heart will heal and you will experience uncontrollable laughter when you feel the power of being completely free.

"If the son, therefore, shall make you free, ye shall be free indeed"

John 8:36

REDVERB: To get something you never had, you need to do something you never did. When God takes away something from your grasp, He's not punishing you but merely opening your hands to receive something better.

"Insanity is defined by doing the same thing repeatedly and expecting a different result."

- *Accept what is, let go of what was and have faith in what will be.*
- *The mountains you are carrying are meant to be climbed*
- *You don't drown by falling in the water you drown by staying there*

Moment of Mirth: A father often read Bible stories to his young children, one day he read, *"The man Lot was warned to take his wife and flee out of the city!"* But his wife looked back and was turned to salt. His son asked, *"What happened to the flea?"*

Quote: Amelia who was four years old was fighting going to sleep. Seth her father and Brigette her mother told her to close her eyes. She said, *"I don't want to close my eyes because that transports you to tomorrow and I'm not ready for tomorrow!"*

TASK #4: Go out and purchase a kite or better yet make one (Kite making instructions on pages 195-201 then wait for a windy day and "Go fly a kite!"

CHAPTER 5

The Mud Puddle

1964

Like most kids in my neighborhood we were poor, so we invented things to do. Almost every day I'd walk over to the Arnold Palmer mini-golf and sweep the greens to play for free. Life can be fun with a whole world to play in and a willingness to find a way.

There were days I felt myself slipping into adulthood, with the troubles we had at home. Hurt by yesterday, scared about today, worrying about tomorrow. Hoping there would be a tomorrow. Even so the future seemed bleak and without hope. I felt the weight of the world as joy became hopelessness. Loneliness was my companion, and he always brought his friend, despair. I tried to be a perfect kid hoping someone would love me. It was easy to forget what it meant to be a kid.

Bruises happen, pain passes but loneliness always sat by my side. It made itself a home in my heart. It's hard to heal when you never stop feeling the pain.

A battle royal broke out in our house one morning. I hid from the possibility of being beaten or even worse becoming part of the quagmire. I waited for the right moment and silent as a ninja wearing sneakers I floated in the air invisible to most humans. I ran as fast as I could from the ensuing war.

Survival was all that mattered. Life was not fun. It was easy to pack away hurt feelings while trying to patch up a broken heart. Feeling like an outsider *"Did I cause all of this?"* Blaming myself for things I had no control of.

I headed out to find my friends. I crossed the street, wading through knee-deep water that came from a recent storm. That seemed to stay inside my house as well.

We lived dark and twisted lives. Running away to the circus could be a solution. Maybe if I wasn't there things would be better. Something had to be done to bring peace to my home and heart.

My clothes were wet from the waist down as I passed the trees across the street. I was looking for the few friends I had. Most of them were involved in the same reality show that I was. We were kindred spirits looking for great adventures that would take us away from all of this.

Behind our sub-division was a pond that always filled up after a rain storm. It was the world's most perfect mud puddle.

I was contemplating jumping in when the gang showed up. No one said anything, we just looked at each other and on a silent secret signal we jumped in.

My friends dealt with the same problems, we all had battles at home. Lonnie my friend and I'd made plans to go to Bora-Bora. We were going to grow pineapples and learn to fire dance.

To institute these grand plans, we'd built a make shift raft and hid it in the trees. First, we'd go to France and then Bora-Bora. We'd built it with branches and scrap pieces of wood we had found. We tested it and were ready to sail down the Chesapeake Bay. To make sure we made it I even secured and old sheet for a sail. But somehow our parents found out about our plans telling us how dangerous it could have been. They didn't know that we had watched every episode of Aqua-Man we knew if we got in trouble he would save us.

Anything would be better than the abuse and pressures we lived under. We'd lost our joy. We were forced to think like an adult to survive. We just wanted to be kids.

Lonnie was the first to jump in and the mud began to fly. I followed him as the rest of our tribe joined in. It wasn't long, until we were completely covered in mud. Mud balls began to hit their targets. Lonnie got hit in the nose, I laughed so hard I forgot to look up and I was destroyed by the biggest piece of mud I had ever seen. All you could see was the whites of our eyes and our teeth when we laughed. The mud slid down our faces the war was on.

This was a full-on mud fight as we played till we could hardly breathe. Soon we just laid there tired and worn out. I was as happy as a squirrel in a nut factory, smiling like a mouse in Wisconsin.

As the day wore on the battle ceased and we headed back to our homes. I found our garden hose in the backyard and started washing off the remnants of the day. The water was warm at first but soon ran colder. I worked a little faster to scrap off all the mud. George S. Patton would have been proud because we were all that we could be.

The water began to clear and as it did I realized that all the panic and fear was gone. Somehow, I had left everything in the mud. As the last piece of mud washed away I felt at peace. As I walked back into my house the realization that things could get rough again hit me. But now I knew there would always be some mud to jump into.

It was weeks before that mud puddle dried up. But then somehow a hose would be turned on and it would fill up again. Every time we went I learned to leave my troubles there. When I washed away the day's mud everything washed away with it. I learned to leave it in the mud.

Each day you live troubles can visit you, the past can haunt you and the future can seem like a place to fear. You need to release each day's challenges if you're going to have faith in the future. Every day when the storm clouds gather give it to the mud. Then wash it off till the water is clear again.

Your enemy is satan. We've identified him and know that his goal is to steal, kill and destroy your dreams, your hopes and the gifts you had as a kid. You must guard what you say and evaluate what you think to eliminate the cynical imaginations that have guided you. Once you give your daily challenges to the mud replace them with powerful imaginations, positive phrases and the promises of God. This brings an awareness of the awesomeness of being a kid in the Kingdom of God. Put away your daily baggage, don't pack again, give it to the mud.

To insure your growth become a servant to those who are embattled and broken themselves. Giving is the core to living. Your confirmation, your complete and total healing is powered by giving to others any truth you've learned. You'll be on your way to becoming a kid again.

But be aware. You wake up and it's Monday. The alarm goes off. You try to wake up and your heart is pounding. You gather yourself together finding the kitchen and that first cup of coffee. That jolt of caffeine helps open your eyes while you're eating breakfast. It's cold and your orange juice is not. You're wishing the day was over before it begins. You can't get out from under *"What's over you."*

The price of gasoline is way up, your income way down. You take a shower, it's cold again. Your spouse spent way to long washing his bald head. You dry off, dress, grab your keys and try to drink the last bit of the second cup of lukewarm coffee that was forsaken on the kitchen counter.

Barely awake, somewhat alive you head to work. You glance at the clock in your car and realize that it's only 5 am. The power went off last night. Reaching for your notes you accidently knock over the last bit of coffee you had left.

Your Monday is like every other Monday. You can't quit your job because the cable will if you do. The pay is tolerable most people are nice. Except Clevis.

Your early and your day starts with a fistful of stress you glance at the quarterly reports they remind you that you forgot to pay a few bills last week. One of them of course was the cable bill.

You've made this wonderful commitment to change and feel a genuine difference in your heart. You eliminated the weight you'd carried. But it's easy to fall back into familiar patterns. They can derail you causing you to limp a little again. Life in all its glory can be tough day-by-day.

Right then, as if Monday hasn't already been a great challenge, Clevis walks by and tells you in a very intimidating way that he's been promoted to be your boss. And of course, he's looking forward to working with you. He's been with the company for a far shorter time than you. In fact, you trained him. You applied for the same job. You knew you should have learned to play golf.

You're tempted to find a small carrying case. One that's not to noticeable. It couldn't hurt to have a small one could it?

This daily battle of life can lead to a lifetime of stolen dreams. It's time to throw in the towel. Every day can be an unbelievable burden and a challenge to your new beliefs.

Nature teaches us many things. If you take a frog and put him in cold water, he will be at peace. If you increase the heat in small increments that frog will sit there without a worry in the world. He will adjust to the heat. Turn the heat up and he will adjust again. The frog will continue to adjust to the heat until it has no power left and is totally worn out. Hotter and hotter until the water boils and he finally croaks.

On the other hand, if you throw a frog into hot water he will react instantly and jump out of that situation. Life can take away your will to win. Doing nothing can bring death to your dreams and potential growth. That's why holding on to that small carrying case can be deadly, you will lose.

Great discoveries and wonderful surprises lay ahead. Life will visit you with uplifting ups and down trodden downs. Every day you need a place to go so when the heat rises you won't stay in the water to long.

Give it to the mud.

Dreams are held onto by moments and then moments become seconds and seconds become minutes as minutes turn into hours. Then hours will eventually become a day lived.

At any given moment, something can go wrong. If you let it that something can steal your joy, rob your vision, and end your dreams. Your heart can fragment again. You live in patterns sometimes falling into ruts and trip on your own intentions. Though it may seem impossible you can pick up your frustrations and pain and If you're not careful you will need an overnight bag again. A broken heart is hard to heal.

Kids are indestructible they will live forever. We must consonantly remind them not to chase a ball into the street. They think only of the moment. They don't think about the past or the future. There too busy living life today. The most positive kid in the world can cry and be hurt. But then there are bikes to ride, marbles to play and mud puddles to find.

It's time to learn the secrets of the mud.

As your day wears on stress, missed appointments, traffic and gaining two pounds can wear you down. Life becomes full of problems. That daily grind makes you feel two foot tall.

There are no such things as problems-Just solutions.

Any problem, big or small, deserves a solution. An enormous problem may seem unsurmountable until you understand that you only need to take that first step to start solving it. Solution based thinking is always better than problem-based worry.

Give it to the Mud!

You make daily decisions about what you'll eat, what you'll wear and what road you'll travel. Life is made up of the decisions you make right or wrong. If you've decided to develop problems and then share them with your friends, then your developing problems. If you show pictures of your problems hold them up for everyone to see. You're creating, expanding even being proud of the problems you have.

Your choices will always dictate what you believe. Your beliefs become the catalyst to run or hate the morning sun. Faith will free us to be us.

Dreams can come true or end by what you believe and conceive. Mastering the art of the mud, when you pray, cast your cares on

Him. Because He cares for you. It's this daily discipline that will help you maintain your child-like heart. His intention is that you'll live a life full of uncompromising joy. The mud will fly, and if you follow through the water will become clear.

The only time you see shadows is if you're in the light always remember that stars still shine in the darkest night. Always share with God who cares the things you cannot bare.

Casting all your care upon Him; for He careth for you.

1 Peter 5:7

God has a boatload of promises for you. He backs up each one if you meet the conditions of that promise. Read them, believe them, receive them.

Jesus is your mud puddle share with Him, give Him your cares and never pick them up again. Real people with real faith in real situations become free by giving it all to God.

There are things in this world that are painful beyond comprehension and can be overwhelming. The world outside has evil stalking the streets like a hungry lion looking for a steak to eat.

God has a plan. That you would be protected under His wings, live a life of joy and peace. That you would understand the power of true love.

That you will become His kid again.

As you give your life to God problems fade and solutions show themselves. God understands the problems in this world and has a solution for each one. But you must accept them to receive them.

REDVERB: God makes the sunshine and the rain if you look hard enough you'll see a mud puddle He has for you. Jump in, leave your problems there.

If what you're doing in life is not working, isn't it time to do something different?

In every heart, there is a need to be a kid again.

You know you have lost your child-hood when you walk around a mud puddle instead of through it.

Just as a reminder:

The trouble with quotes on the internet is that you can never know if they're genuine.

Abraham Lincoln

YOUR 5TH SECRET MISSION

1. Give your troubles and cares away, every day.

2. Hold onto nothing, give up everything, believe in the things that lift you up that don't hold you down.

3. Read and find the promises of God in the Bible. Internalize them, speak them, live them, understand them.

One of the devil's best tricks is to take an episode of failure and turn it into a three-act play of despair. Bringing death to your vision, your dreams, your life. With you in the starring role forgetting your lines. He hasn't written a comedy but a dark sad tragedy. He's hoping you'll give in and your life will become a one-act play.

1989

I recall the pain, the emotions, the darkness. Surrounded by despair and depression so powerful I was willing to do anything to stop it. I remember it all.

No matter what I tried, failure happened. Nothing worked. Lonely, depressed and desperate to find a way out. I thought of ending my life. My battles with the devil had become intense. And unfortunately, I was trying to fix everything myself. God sat on the sidelines waiting for me to call but I had lost everything including His number.

During the summer I was driving down Highway forty in an eighty-five thousand-pound 18-wheeler full of cargo. The great part of that summer my daughter rode with me on a new summer program for kids for parents who drove. Even if everything else wasn't working my kids were everything to me. And the only thing good in my life at that time.

We were driving in Texas when my daughter saw a sign for free kittens and before the day had ended she talked me into getting one. We named him Dallas a six-month old Tabby that treated the truck like its own personal kingdom roaming around as we drove from state to state.

I had turned a corner onto a very dangerous road where hope could not be found on any map. We pulled into a local truck stop to rest. It had been a tiring day. Rachel and Dallas had fallen asleep on the bottom bunk. She was so happy. My beautiful little girl, I was so blessed to have her in my life. But the shadows had brought darkness and at that moment I couldn't sleep.

I was at the end of my rope, conflicted and hurting. I didn't know how much more my broken heart would take.

Standing outside the truck I locked the doors making sure that my daughter was safe. I began to walk, I walked all night trying to deal with my emotions. I had known the Lord for many years but somehow had moved away from Him. I no longer heard His voice deaf to all I had heard and blind to all that I had read. Despondent needing relief, I started to think about how to end it all.

The easiest way I thought was to drive this eighty-five-thousand-pound truck into a concrete bridge after I had taken my daughter and Dallas home.

I had seen incredible moments of faith in my life. Miracles and amazing times watching God move in incredible ways. But if you're not careful life can overtake when your enemy whispers his lies and deceptions. Trying to fight Him without God is like jumping into a pool of Piranhas carrying a rare steak in your hands. You think you can handle it but realize your mistake too late.

The devil will do everything he can to stop anyone that challenges him. At that moment in my life he was winning.

I cried all night, tired from the struggle. I headed back towards the truck and then the thought hit me. *What would my daughter do without me? What about my boys?* My fatherly instincts began to take over. And I knew I couldn't do this to them. It was then that I decided no matter how deep the pain was, nothing would be worth hurting my kids.

A fog began to lift I was under an incredible attack from my enemy. I could see a small glimpse of light as it started to shine within me. It felt like I was wiping off a dirty mirror.

I got myself back together and climbed back into the truck my daughter was still laying there peacefully with her new pet snuggled next to her.

I don't know if it's possible to put this into words. But I never loved anything like this little girl and my two boys. They were everything to me. I would gladly lay down my life for them without a thought. There's a spiritual connection that cannot be severed once you hold them, love them and raise them. The only thing that saved me that night was remembering that I was a dad. It was my happy thought this amazing love I have for them.

I never had a dad in my life. I don't know what it would have felt like to have one. I never had the experience. But I was now a father, and nothing meant more to me than that. During my early life it was my mother's love and determination that helped me make it. My sister, brother and I wouldn't have made it without her.

She was our shining angel. There are few people that have overcome so much but still believe in tomorrow. There were times when I'm sure she wanted to give up, but my mom is one tough broad. I inherited that from her.

1991

After that summer I asked God to help me understand the path that had gotten me so close to destruction. And how to find my way back to Him. He told me to drive to a beach early in the morning some 150 miles away and wait for Him there.

Father spoke, I listened.

The only sound at the beach was a piercing silence. It was ominous, transforming. It had no manner, form or reason; seconds became minutes as the hours passed away. Eventually the dawning sun rose above the horizon and lit fire to the Atlantic Ocean, consuming, enveloping the beach I was on. The waves like sentinels forced their way to shore, lapping up what remained of a shallow beach. The calm, rhythmic sea was calling the sand back to a place where only mermaids play. As the ocean breeze captured the sea Mother ocean danced with Father sky.

At 4:00 a.m. uncomfortable and lonely, I sat there in the darkest part of the beach, drinking cold coffee while my Egg Mc muffin sat beside me, catching cold from exposure, partially eaten almost forgotten. I was bundled up in half starched sheets with the full comprehension of my sad and troubled spirit.

God told me to come here to witness the birth of this new day. I had been torn and twisted by the loss of my marriage and the daily presence of my children.

My broken heart was apparent.

Earlier that year, my eleven-year marriage had ended. It was a storm of a marriage she dealt with bi-polar manic depression and I dealt with how to handle it. We certainly cared for each other, having had three children, but no matter how hard we tried, it seemed that there was no way to fix what was broken. There was no bi-polar manic depression book for dummies. If there had been, I would have read it.

In the middle of all my turmoil, looking for answers God told me to drive to this beach. To wake up early in the morning, get a cup of coffee and wait for the sunrise. I had no idea why, but I tend to listen to my Father's advice. In the process I told a few friends what God had told me to do and they decided to follow along.

When we got there, they partied all night. They said that they would join me in the morning. But a 2 a.m. drunk doesn't make a 4 a.m. appointment with God very easy. I sat there dark and alone.

I don't know what stupid decision I'd made that had led to this life, but I felt as lost and weak as the sand. I wondered what would be next. It was cold, dark, why this place? What purpose does this serve? Dead for so long, finding nothing, seeing nothing, hoping for nothing, feeling nothing.

My coffee grew colder and my Egg Mc Muffin looked sad, cold and lonely as it sat there waiting for the sun to rise. Seagulls started their daily ritual of bobbing and weaving with the currents of the cool morning breeze seeking eatable remains left over from the previous day. They cackled and screeched flying so close at times I could feel the flapping of their wings.

Big dirt movers and heavy equipment roamed the beach like massive big bulls belching smoke from their nostrils snorting out loud. They were giving voice to their deep complaints about the never-ending job they were employed to do. They worked hard to replace the sand that the ocean had taken back; big impressive dump trucks did their best to fill the apparent loss from the last storm. As they worked to repair the void, the dirt movers pushed around everything in their path fighting to reclaim what was stolen. Their proud, often clamorous sounds were only interrupted by the continual march of the ocean to the shore, working against all their efforts.

I felt their frustration but admired their tenacity.

Suddenly things changed. It began so innocently; the darkness showed signs of giving up the grip of the night. The light so softly invaded the darkness as it ran away from the light as if it was on fire. The waves took on a sparkling display of color and light it began to warm the sand around me. When it reached me, I felt the embracing warmth of the sun. It came over me like a beautiful comfortable quilt. I felt it's warmth as it reached inside my cold, broken heart, something began to change, it felt like a heavy closed door was opening. The rusty lock clanging, falling to the earth. I cried uncontrollably; time stopped as the sun broke through the horizon.

I was encompassed by the overwhelming presence of God. He reached deep inside my spirit and pulled me close to Him, as close as a whisper. Then came His voice, *"My son, I give you another day."* It was earth-shattering; it was hope defined.

I had lost all hope but there it was in the sand on that beach, illuminated by the dawning sun. Hope is hard to find once you lost it. No matter how hard you try or by what means you use to secure it, once lost, it's lack will take away every gift you had as a child.

But there it was again like a hidden pirate treasure lit up by the rays of the sun. There would be another day. He told me to forget the past, the failure, the broken dreams because He had a brand-new future for me. I just had to believe and receive it. My broken heart began to heal and for the first time in a very long time I began to feel His love.

Every morning since then when the sun rises I remember that beach and that sand, the sunrise that morning my cold coffee and warming heart. My gifts had been renewed and rekindled, I began to feel like a kid again as the child within me stood up. The dawn eliminated every dark thought I had and was leading me into an amazing new adventure.

When I cry now it's for the utter joy I feel. I can't contain it. He kept His promise. Hope restored my faith, faith bolstered my gift of love and love brought me to a place of joy. Joy so complete I feel the sun shining even in the rain.

I learned to let go and rebuild my dreams. Proverbs says a hope deferred makes one sick. But if you trust Him He will fulfill what you desire. He will give you a tree of life. Obeying God has taught me more than I can ever fathom.

Hope deferred maketh the heart sick: but when the desire cometh, it is a tree of life.

Trust *in the Lord, and do good; so shalt thou dwell in the land, and verily thou shalt be fed.*

Delight *thyself also in the Lord: and He shall give thee the desires of thine heart.*

Commit *thy way unto the Lord, also trust in Him, and He shall bring it to pass.*

*And He shall bring forth thy righteousness as the **light**, and thy judgement as for the noon day.*

Rest in the Lord and wait patiently for Him: fret not thyself because of him who prospereth in his way, because of the man who bringeth wicked devices to pass.

Cease from anger and forsake wrath: fret not thyself in any wise to do evil.

Proverbs 13:12

Joy came in the morning, as the light broke through.

All God's promises are conditional, there spiritual laws that must be followed to become effective. You've heard that you need to stay away from sin, what that really means is to stay away from satan's influence. The laws God has put into place are there to protect you. The devil can steal your desires, your hopes and your dreams. *"Trust in the Lord, do good, delight thyself in the Lord, commit your ways to Him, rest in Him, wait patiently for Him, cease from anger, forsake wrath, do no evil."*

For the wages of sin is death; but the gift of God is eternal life through Jesus Christ our Lord.

Romans 6:23

Death to your dreams, your hopes, your very life.

This is how you find the true desires of your heart. The devil will do everything to trip you up. He'll convince you that God is not listening. The truth is, God hurts to see His child (you) remain in a place that He cannot reach because you've walked away from Him. If you follow the world you would fail. Follow God and you'll succeed.

In His favor is life: weeping may endure for a night, but joy cometh in the morning

Psalm 30:5

The beginning of a new day can bring hope, a new beginning, a new life. Every new day is a promise waiting to happen.

The Tree of Life can be found if you seek it. Once the light shines the sun rises as the shadows of the past fade away. Living a spiritual life is the journey to understanding why, how, when and where.

Eternity rests in your soul, and if you allow it, transforms you by reforming your spirit. You become a new creature, all things become new. It's a powerful, all-consuming, life changing moment when you yield to the Spirit of God. By saying *"God be my God, heal me, renew me, become one with me,"* Your physiology changes, you react to the world differently, you speak differently. You see a new light, a new dawn, an eternal flame. It sanctifies you helps you rectify the past and as God's love encompasses you the world and its battles melt away.

But as you walk into the light as He is in the light your enemy satan tries to fight you tooth and nail. It's his wish that you stay tired embattled and bound by this world. That you still fight in the flesh instead of the spirit. It's his plan to stop you from really understanding the promises and weapons of God. He'll do anything he can to keep you from receiving the power that comes from unifying your soul, mind and body with the Spirit of God.

We are created in His image. When you take on God as your king and Lord you put on His unbendable armor. The only time you'll be vulnerable is when you listen to satan and take the armor off. Jesus changed the world we live in because He yielded to His father's calling. Totally committed to His mission. The more you yield to God the more powerful you become. Your mind, your will, your emotions are solid as steel. The world takes on a whole new color as you see with the eyes of an angel, hear with the ears of a saint, and comprehend life as a child.

Allow Him to love you, forgive you and teach you. Your strength will increase beyond your wildest dreams. You've tapped into eternity and a power source that won't be moved unless you allow it. Spirit, soul and body become one, just like the trinity. Because your mind has yielded to the spiritual Kingdom of God that now lives inside you. You become more powerful than any battle you may face.

In the past you may have thought He turned away from you forever, but nothing is farther from the truth. He was there during my darkest hours; He was the closest He had ever been to me.

While I struggled in the darkness He brought me to a place where the new dawning sun shined the light. On that beach He said to me *"I'm here son, here's my gift to you."* I had given up, but at that moment like the great Father He is I felt a surge of His love and compassion for me. He kept His promise.

It got me through my past, taught me the incredible truth of *"Now"* and gave me hope for the future. To this day whenever I experience the sun rising these many years later I see His hand extended. I feel His heart sharing the love of a good Father. It reminds me of His promise. Because life has been amazing since that day on the beach.

He established a promise and kept it. And when life kicks me around at times my hope has held, and I have become more than a conqueror. I'm ready to play, willing to stay each and every day.

Gathering together my now hung-over friends, we left the motel and headed home. They looked like death warmed over I felt I had entered a new world. Everything looked brighter; I was overcome by His presence and love.

I have fought other battles since then but then the sun rises, and I'm given one more day. Joy has become an ever-present part of my life, and love has taken residence in my heart and soul. I live each day like it will be my last because some day I will be right.

The battles teach you, the hard choices test you and the terrifying hurdles can slow you down. But if you hold on, listen to His voice you will not only dictate the kind of life you now live, you'll dominate those challenges. You'll become an even greater version of yourself as you open your spirit to truth and love.

If you're not having fun, then you should, because the truth is fun, and fun is good. **RED**

Casting all your care upon Him; for He careth for you.

1 Peter5:7

"*Live each day as if it were your last...because one day, you'll be right.*"

REDVERB: "*What could you accomplish if you knew you could not fail?*"

Moment of Mirth: Two priests are standing by the side of the road holding up a sign that reads "*The end is near!*" *Turn yourself around now before it's too late!*" They desperately hold up the sign to every passing car. "*Leave me alone, you religious nuts!*" yells the first driver as he speeds by, from around the curve, the priest hears screeching tires and a big splash. "*Do you think,*" one priest says to the other, it would be better to shorten the sign to say, "*Bridge Out*" instead?"

Task#5: Find a mud-puddle. You know what to do next.

Bonus gift #1:

Solving the problems in life involves a crucial task. Solve the puzzle below to learn what that step is.

R _ _ _ _ _ E _ _!!!

What does it say? (Answer on page 220)

CHAPTER

6

Sour Pickles

It's Saturday morning and you've looked forward to sleeping in. But the sun invaded your room and rudely woke you up. Your stomach's growling you feel like you haven't eaten in weeks. You fold back the blanket pick the pillows off the floor and head towards the kitchen. The traditional offerings don't intrigue you much. You're looking for something exotic and different. No typical food will do and for some reason, all you can think about is pickles.

You walk half-awake, fully aware that you'd saw something special in the refrigerator the night before. You head towards the kitchen and open the refrigerator as the cool air brushes past your face. You move the month-old milk and the day-old hamburger, there they are, on the top shelf you see them pickles. Sweet and sour, dill pickles, hot pickles, and then you see it a brand-new jar of sour pickles.

You don't recognize the brand and its red label gives you a feeling of worry, the name makes you pause. *"The World's Sourest Pickles"* before you pick them up you look around to make sure there is no audience. As you pick up the jar you wonder" Am *I up for the challenge?"* You like living on the edge, consider yourself a real man, not afraid of anything. Could this be the time that you take on too much?

But then you remember that your kids call you *"Mr. Danger"* and that's way cool! So, you stand tall, carry the jar to the kitchen table poised for adventure at every turn a man of mystery and intrigue. Yes, I am *"Mr. Danger"* no pickle will get the best of me!

You take a minute to look around making sure no one is hiding around the corner. You're not sure how you'll react to eating this new delicacy. The jar seems heavier than expected and there is a warning label.

"These are the sourest pickles known to man. Developed from a recipe found in King Tut's Crypt in the Valley of the Kings. Created as a punishment for those who blasphemed the king." This doesn't scare you, but the skull and crossbones printed in blood red gives you pause. You laugh, thinking to yourself *"Really? They can't be that bad!"*

You've been warned but you've been here before. And you don't even flinch.

You've taken on greater challenges than these before. You always thought that 007 had nothing on you. Remember eating that 72-ounce steak in Amarillo, Texas? Or the four-pound burger and fries in Arizona including an 84-ounce Pepsi?

No sour pickle is going to get the best of you. You shake the jar a little to make sure it doesn't explode you begin to open the jar there's a small hissing sound, it sounds like a cobra ready to strike. The thought crosses your mind *"Great Marketing!"*

Your hands shake as you open the jar. The lid parts from the jar and an evil smell invades the room something you've never encountered before. You look at the jar making sure it isn't out of date. Holding the jar away from your body you start to put the lid back on when out of nowhere your two boys, wife and neighbors come into the kitchen.

The mist from the jar left a rancid smell that overcomes them. Everyone begins to back up trying to escape its effect. Your wife says, *"Honey!?!"* You look at her and say, *"It's the pickles, it's not me!"* She looks at you in disbelief until she sees the jar in your hands.

She giggles *"I bought those, never thinking anyone would be brave enough to eat one. But then I knew you were a man of intrigue a real super hero!"* she starts laughing a little.

Your trying hard to put the lid back on without anyone noticing, but it doesn't seem to want to go back on.

But then your son speaks up *"That's no problem for my dad! Remember the time dad ate fifty-five nuclear hot wings in fifteen minutes? This will be nothing for him!"* Your shoulders slump as you realize there is no turning back. You can't let your boys down. You put the jar down on the table with care, grab a plate and a glass to get something to drink. You carefully take the lid off the jar. It's as if someone has released an atom bomb powered by the smell of a five-day old dead skunk. The smell makes your lips quiver. Your mouth waters a bead of sweat forms on your forehead, your hands shake again.

You wonder if you should call to increase your life insurance, run like the wind or just do it. But you know the answer you can't help yourself. You take a moment to adjust your chair just in case you faint. You take a fork and stab a pickle. The juice from the jar and the newly purloined pickle hits your hand and splashes on the table- *"Is that eating a hole in the table?"* You turn away as fast as possible. But you know you must go through with it.

You're dizzy, experiencing a maximum amount of pickle overload. Holding tight to the corner of the table; your hand trembles uncontrollably, your feet slip as you try to adjust and prepare for what's ahead. You mumble a quick prayer something about last rites.

Before you take a bite, your body reacts to this unusual snack. You're imagining the effects before they even happen. Your mouth has now filled with saliva and your mind takes over. The situation is now very real as your body reacts before you even take a bite.

You slice the pickle and the juices from the pickle take the varnish off your plate. The aroma is the sourest thing you have ever smelled. It has enveloped the entire area, everyone backs up from the offending odor. "Why *did my wife buy these?*" You wonder.

But you're a real man, right? You knew they should have picked you to play Indiana Jones. Your wife sees your panic and starts to reach for these overpowering portions of destruction. But then pulls back, thinking "*I can't, this is going to be too much fun!*"

Your sons begin to yell "Go, *dad, go!*" You bring the pickle towards your mouth, Saliva has built up like the Pacific Ocean, your life flashes before your eyes. As you crunch down on this sour pickle, the juices fill your mouth your taste buds scream out "*Were not your buds anymore!*"

Your tongue runs away from the onslaught, it takes every bit of strength to bite down on this unusual food. You're in a pickle now! Every fiber in your being is saying "*Spit it out*" But you can't have your boys seeing you quit. *"No, man up!"* you say to yourself.

You see visions of heaven "*Is that Jesus calling me home?*" All the built-up saliva has dried up and disappeared. Your mouths on fire! You grab for the glass in front of you, but you forgot to get water! You run to the sink standing on your tippy toes drinking straight from the faucet as everyone is laughing.

The water gives you some relief enough to put the lid on the pickles in case they could cause an unknown malady to your family. You get a standing ovation as you throw what remains of the pickles in the trash.

Your knees are weak, you can hardly stand but in an act of defiance you throw your fist up in the air as you fall to the floor in a dead faint.

Imagination is a powerful tool for good or evil, it's the core of faith or failure. As you read this story your mouth began to water. You experienced the same type of physical response as the dad did. Even though you were not there. Your imagination took over you could feel what it felt like to eat those pickles.

Let's do an experiment of our own. Find a comfortable chair sit down and relax. Close your eyes and clear your mind. In front of you is a juicy tart lemon, imagine grabbing it, trying to peel it.

The rind refuses to come off the lemon, the little bit you have peeled off causes the air to be filled with the scent of the lemon. The smell of the lemon is tart with an acid finish. You bring the lemon towards your face which intensifies the smell as you react to its powerful odor. Without stopping you bite into the lemon right through the peeling. The juice from the lemon runs down your face. The bitterness and tart flavor of the lemon invades your senses as you bite down on the lemon.

Your mouth began to water as if you were biting the lemon, there was no lemon, there was no bitterness, but you felt it and could feel the effects of it. It was real as if you did it.

You've been given a powerful gift imparted to you at an early age. Everyone has this gift. It's the most powerful gift of its kind. With this gift, you can climb Mt. Everest, fly to the moon or sing at Radio City Music Hall. You can make a bright day black, an excellent trip unbearable or your life an unescapable bottomless pit.

God gave us the gift of imagination to use as a powerful weapon to succeed. It uses was to imagine how beautiful life can be. The deceiver understands this, he uses it to corrupt your life, helping you imagine that your future will be filled with unrelenting pain and despair.

God's intention was that it would be the gateway to see and believe a bright future, building your dreams, fulfilling your wishes. Worry, chaos, unpaid bills that strange sound you hear as you start your car become tools for the devil to exploit. You can use this powerful tool to amplify the positive or magnify the negative. Imagination can rectify and glorify your past, present, and your future.

Your world is created by what you believe. If your gift of imagination is being used correctly then you can see a fantastic future before you even get there. Believing that great days are ahead activates your imagination and substantiates that belief. You heard others say, *"I will believe it when I see it!"* Using your imagination, the way God intended, and you will *"Believe it and then see it."*

As kids, we saw the world through imagination. We were super heroes saving the day or cowboys out on the range. Our vision was so real that others believed it and soon were fighting train robbers and saving the day with our super hero powers.

But then we got older and our imagination began seeing other possibilities. *"What if I can't pay the rent? I'm feeling a little sick must be the yellow fever! I know she's going to leave me."* Imagination can stir up hope, faith, love, peace and even joy. Or it can create greed, jealousy, hate, prejudice, depression and satan's favorite fear.

It can be dark in the middle of the brightest day and become impossible to get out of bed. Completely corrupting the original intention that God had for your imagination. Seeing your future as an exciting, interesting, place where you live free and full of life.

REDVERB: **Worry is the misuse of your imagination**

You have the power to change everything. Begin by forming a vision of what and where you want to be.

Imagine for a moment that you envision a beautiful dream home. The walls come together, the roof put on. You see the colors you want to paint with, the type of furniture you would have. And there in front of you is a staircase made with a beautiful rare wood.

Your imagination kicks into high gear now and the kitchen is complete, the bathrooms are lovely. Your vision, your imagination starts bringing all of this to life. You see your house sitting on a beautiful hill overlooking a waterfall. Your building this beautiful home in your mind. As you open your eyes in front of you is the actual house you dreamed of. Somehow, you've built it.

Your vision is complete as you imagined it. With amazement you walk towards the house. How is this possible? You walk into the house, what an incredible power to have. You touch the walls and look over the valley and say to yourself, *"Why stop there!"*

You close your eyes imagining the type of car you want, the spouse you would like, your new beautiful children Purvis and Cletus and don't forget cute little Bessie Mae. Don't stop now, you're on a roll how about that French bulldog you always wanted *"Clyde!"* Whoops, he just peed on the floor. No worries your imagination quickly finds a mop.

You're amazed at all you see. It's unreal. Whatever you use your imagination for is manifested. It takes your breath away as you dreamt it and imagined it, it becomes reality for you.

You take a few moments to catch your breath as you gaze upon a beautiful blue sky watching the birds fly towards the sun. Your vision is exact and complete in detail. *"Why didn't I use this incredible power before?"* So, then you imagine a private movie theater with a brand new 450-inch super HD7 flat screen TV with Dolby Surround Sound powered by a 457-engine pumping out bass that can shatter glass! As you eat popcorn from your new concession stand.

And then you realize, wait a minute, there is a world of need. You begin to see world peace, hunger becoming extinct, the powerful force of God's love released to help a dark and hurting world. And you know in your heart that this is far more important than any house you could have dreamt of.

You begin to use this new power to find ways to change the world making it a better place, to see a real change in the lives of others. And right before your eyes children are no longer crying but are laughing, playing, happy, no longer hungry as God intended in the first place. You weep with joy.

Where do you believe the universe we live in came from? Where do you think cats, flowers, trees and the ocean began? God imagined them, and He created everything you see. He imparted to us His greatest power the power of imagination.

God said, *"Let us make man in our image"* His intention was for us to be like Him. To be creators Like Him. Enabling us to use the power of His creative mind.

The power of imagination has created every cure and written every book. Before it hit the big screen, every movie, every scene was filmed by using the power of imagination.

Imagination has built bridges where there were walls, highways where there we no roads. Imagination has changed the world we live in tearing away the chains of slavery, giving us the ability to fly, creating a world of love and hope by cutting away the roots of hate, bitterness and despair.

It can create genuine love and give vision to those blinded by the world. Those who could not see can now see through the power of imagination a world full of color and music beyond any person with 20/20 vision. By using this great gift of imagination.

You just experienced it as you reacted to a story that became an image in your mind. As the dad bit into that pickle and you bit into that lemon it became so real that your body reacted as if it was really happening to you at that moment.

The power of your mind to create is fantastic! It was what God intended from the beginning and this gift can give life or take it away.

Your enemy will warp this gift showing you how to misuse this gift through worry. The gift of imagination, like many of God's gifts, has been twisted and manipulated by the devil and his crew to make you focus on what can go wrong instead of what can go right.

It was given to show us how to win the war, to fly like an eagle soaring high reaching new levels of success. The devil traps you making you believe that you'll never leave the ground, powerless to fight any battle.

Children were born equipped for the battle with an incredible, unshakeable faith that would humble most Biblical Prophets. A never-ending source of love with a tremendous ability to cope with life, A system so powerful that even the most abused child can imagine a brighter future.

Kids see the world through different eyes. They learn at an accelerated rate far beyond any adult. They dance in public and laugh without reason. Nothing is more day-changing than hearing a baby laugh.

To become a kid again, you need to use imagination for positive, powerful images that build you up and never tear you down. As a kid you could fly, drive the fastest car in a race and even believe in Leprechauns.

Born with a giving spirit, kids are wide open to the positive possibilities of this world. Their faith is resolute. We live in a scary world full of pain and abuse. It goes without saying that children brought into a world of abuse are different. They take their first steps into adulthood before they enjoyed Saturday morning cartoons and Lucky Charms.

This drives them to grow up fast adapting and changing giving up all their gifts way to early. Their imagination is their greatest enemy as life causes them to enter adulthood at an early age.

Because of abuse, you may not remember being a kid due to the adult situations you encountered. You may have survived but you may still be broken.

You need to fix those feelings and emotions by putting imagination to its greatest work. By Imagining a brighter more vibrant future by leaving the past behind. That past that held you captive and encapsulated your spirit, will and emotions.

Hast thou not known? Hast thou not heard, that the everlasting God, the Lord, the Creator of the ends of the earth, fainteth not, neither is weary? There is no searching of His understanding. He giveth power to the faint, and to them that have no might He increaseth strength. Even the youths shall faint and be weary, and the young men shall utterly fall: But they that wait upon the Lord shall RENEW their strength; they shall mount up with wings as eagles; they shall run, and not be weary, and they shall walk, and not faint.

Isaiah 40:28-31

Worry, fear, and stress are all components of a misused imagination. You built your beautiful home with the power of imagination, but you can tear it down the same way you built it. By letting your enemy instill worry and fear in your mind. Making you believe there is no structure that is safe. Your home destroyed, your life in disarray.

Those who imagine the worst can compromise their physical health by dwelling on how bad things can be. Imagination is meant to be used to destroy any negative thought and bring any stressful situation to the ground. As we have learned taking inventory is the key to identifying the areas that are being used by your imagination.

REDVERB: Worry is the misuse of your imagination.

What kind of house are you building? What kind of life? Does your home need repair, are the windows broken and shattered? Are you in a dry, arid desert, parched land with no water to drink? No breeze to cool you? Reality is what you bring to life. If you imagine the worst, you get the worst. But if you believe the best, then your home will be safe.

Of all the gifts that children possess the power of imagination is the open door to believing the impossible, experiencing the unbelievable and living beyond all short comings they may have. If you're not careful you can create a cynical world filled with sleepless nights and unyielding stress. Believing starts the process of creating. What will you create today? What would happen if you used your imagination to create a positive future? How would your life change? **What could you accomplish if you knew you could not fail?**

The Formula to identify and rectify your thought process

C.A.N.T: Continual Annoying Negative Thoughts

C.A.N: Conquering Annoying Negativity

A wise man once said "*Son, there is no such word as can't.*" That didn't make sense. My family ate dinner from the can marked "*Can't*"

It was a metaphor for our life. "*I can't no sooner do that than bring a greased pig to an opera.*" Not only did we speak it, we believed it.

You can have thoughts reminding you of past mistakes or help create future fear, even panic filled immediate failure. The secret is to identify them, catalog them, rectify them and finalize them. Once you learn what c**an't** means and how to replace it with **can** you will never again say "*I can't, and I won't*" Instead you'll replace it with "*I can, and I will.*"

The Future

Suppose you were asked to perform a task you knew would be a challenge. It's weeks off but you begin to imagine failing. Soon this C.A.N.T thought overtakes you. It's future based, it's a thought that will limit you from growing and learning. "*What if I mess up, what if I fail?*"

It's not real because it hasn't even happened yet! It's time to conquer annoying negativity. Identify this thought as a "*Can't thought*" understand that it is not real. And then reimagine this task as successful and yourself not only doing well but completing the task with excellence. Practice the task, make a daily plan to activate, and understand every facet of the task and then put it into play. This will help you gain the confidence to feel comfortable and perform that task on a whole new level.

You have a choice, creating by your personal beliefs. Take inventory write down every instance where you hear yourself doubting or living in fear of the future. Once you have eliminated the *can't* replace it with *can.*

Evil stalks the streets, we live in a cynical world. At times everywhere, we turn lives are ruined and people have just given up. While the devil runs wild. We live in a can't world. But you can create a "can" world no matter what is happening around you.

The Past

There's regret, unforgiveness, jealousy or dealing with some long-ago event. This next CANT thought deals with the past, you feel that there's nothing that can be done about it, but these thoughts can constantly spring up. These thoughts can stop you from moving on to greater heights of glory, deeper love and a new freedom from pain. Like an anchor it holds you in a position that can destroy or delay any hope of a brighter future. Identify them, catalog them, then rectify them. As you do you will finalize them, because you CAN.

The Immediate CANT

The immediate CANT thought can be the hardest to solve. Faced with a decision that is immediate your first feeling is *"I can't do this"*. Take a breath stop the **continual annoying negative thoughts (C.A.N.T.)** concentrate on your immediate problems and situations as they present themselves. But then put into play the process of **conquering annoying negativity (C.A.N.)** changing the way you deal with these three areas will change the course of your life.

It may be foreign at first but once applied, anything is possible. There is no such word as **can't** because you **can**.

REDVERB: The power of C.A.N. linked with a powerful, positive imagination will help you survive and thrive.

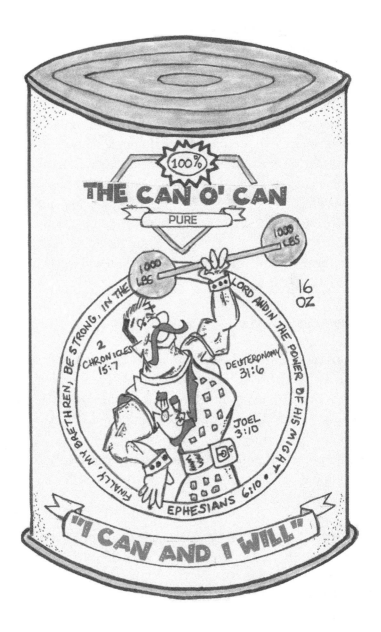

YOUR 6TH SECRET MISSION

1. Identify, rectify and simplify your life by using your imagination to build a bright new future.

2. Eliminate can't and solidify can.

3. Realize that you are a creator then be aware of what you are creating.

Henry David Thoreau said, *"Go confidently in the direction of your dreams, LIVE the life you have imagined."* What kind of life have you imagined?

Getting control of your life means getting a hold of your life. Identify where you are and where you want to be. You have within your grasp the knowledge of God and His kingdom. Speak life, what you speak creates the world you live in.

Don't be limited by what others say and do. Don't be limited by your present situation. Don't let money, your job, your family or your friends define you. Follow your dreams. Live the life you have imagined.

"Imagination is more important than knowledge"

Albert Einstein- (Quoted by George Sylvester Viereck in "What life means to Einstein," *The Saturday Evening Post, Oct 26th, 1929*

"You can't depend on your eyes when your imagination is out of focus"

Mark Twain

*"Don't **RELIVE** your past, **REIMAGINE** your future"* **Red Devine**

"Imagination rules the world." **Napoleon Bonaparte**

"*Imagination is the voice of God. If there is anything God-Like about God, it is that He dared to imagine everything."* **Henry Miller**

Imagination is the preview of life's coming attractions. What God has imagined for you goes way beyond your wildest dreams.

Moment of Mirth: There were kids lined up at a local orphanage getting ready to eat lunch. One little girl walked by a big basket of apples she noticed a sign that read *"Remember only take one apple. God is watching you!"*

As she went further down the line, there was a big basket of cookies. She told the kid in front of her, *"Take all the cookies you want, God's busy watching the apples!"*

TASK #6: Create something, paint a picture, draw, make a sculpture, take a pottery class. Write a song, tell a story. Follow your dreams but be careful to take inventory of every thought. Take the dark thoughts and bring them into the light. Take the wrong and make it right.

CHAPTER

7

Empirical Evidence

S cientists the world over are working on answering the biggest questions concerning life. Where did we come from? How did we get here? And what are the chances that our earth became what it is today?

One of the leading theories of the beginnings of time is the "BIG BANG THEORY." From the research that has been completed they believe there was nothing, and then there was something. Four main elements Hydrogen 75%-Helium about 25%-and about 0.01% of deuterium, and hlium-3 with trace amounts of lithium combined and that recipe made our universe.

One fundamental question that needs to be answered is where did these elements come from? We went from nothing to something, total emptiness to a world full of miracles and wonders. What are the odds that these elements came together and created the world we inhabit? Believing that takes real faith.

When you plant a seed in the ground and it's raised in the right conditions it will grow. But you need someone to plant the seed, create the dirt, water it and care for it. If no one plants the seed, there is no plant, there is no life.

There are many theories about creation and scientist always work toward one goal Empirical Evidence. The day when a theory becomes a fact. I applaud their efforts and have researched many of their findings.

The key to understanding this process is to create a format that will lead to a conclusion. Once you have postulated the evidence it's time to share your findings.

I believe I've found the empirical evidence that proves the existence of God and His influence on designing our world. Evidence that should be published throughout scientific journals world-wide for all to read. It happened one day when I was eating "*The food of the Gods*"

My evidence is supported by the fact that it would take a brilliant, caring creator to take the time to put on this earth the ingredients needed to make brownies.

Someone, somewhere paid close attention to detail when He included everything we need to enjoy this tremendous, wonderful treat. It's hard to believe that what we have on our planet was a throw of the dice. I feel the warmth of the sun and how the wind makes the trees dance and sway. The beauty of this earth is breathtaking and supports billions of people, animals and everything that swims in the sea.

Obviously, someone took their time to make sure we had air to breathe water to drink and an earth that can grow our food. But even with the astronomical equation it would take to create it and the unrelenting facts we see I have one question "*Why are there brownies?*"

Once you have taken that first taste of this Heavenly treat you will be a believer. And if you add Vanilla ice cream you will have an out of body experience and comprehend the Divine. By adding Pecans, whipped cream and hot fudge you'll feel that you have touched the face of God. So, let's look at the facts and see if you can agree with my findings. To make brownies you need seven different items:

1. *Butter*

2. *Salt*

3. *Sugar*

4. *Cocoa powder*

5. *Flour*

6. *Baking Soda*

7. *Eggs*

In our period of discovery, we need to ask, *"Where did all these ingredients come from?"* Delving into the mysteries of brownies consider how impressive it is to not only find these ingredients but how to combine them. It's a worldwide effort to gather the needed items to make this Heavenly treat.

The first ingredient comes from a small village in Central America, a little boy who lives there works with his family on their cacao farm. They have been harvesting cacao for generations. Known as the *"Theobroma"* tree which means "Food of the Gods" these trees are quite fragile. You can't harvest these football shaped pods by climbing the trees. So, this little boy's dad would pick him up to cut the pods off the trunks of these trees. They process them and prepare them for transport. Seventy percent of all cacao pods are grown in Africa, but Central and South America continue to be large producers of cacao.

Each pod contains thirty to forty seeds that are milky white sweet and tart at the same time. Picked twice a year, the cacao seeds are covered with banana leaves and left to ferment in the sun for a week. They are then packed and shipped to chocolate plants throughout the world. Roasted in ovens they are then cracked and opened, inside is the nib that contains the chocolate were looking for. It's then pressed in massive hydraulic presses that crush the nibs into a paste until the cocoa butter is extracted. What's left after this process is a fine powder called cocoa powder.

Then will need vanilla. Its survival is nothing more than a miracle. Without the Melipeone bee there would be no vanilla. Vanilla comes from the only orchid that produces an edible substance. It's grown in Mexico, the Bourbon Islands, Tahiti, Indonesia, India, Uganda and Papua, New Guinea.

In Tahiti families have raised these Orchids for generations and in the past, they had to be pollinated by this one bee. Without the Melipeone bee there would be no vanilla.

People have now learned how to hand pollinate the plants, to hand harvest and cure them. But there would be no plant to hand pollinate without that original miraculous symbiotic relationship. They work with the beans until they are processed it takes thirteen to fourteen weeks to complete this task.

It's then that they ship them to milling machines in manufacturing plants like the one in Waukegan, Illinois. It takes about thirteen ounces of vanilla beans to make one gallon of vanilla extract. It's then bottled and shipped throughout the world.

To make sure your brownies are the best they can be we'll need sugar. This comes from two primary sources: sugar cane and sugar beets. Sugar cane is primarily grown in Polynesia where it got its beginning.

Sugar beets are grown throughout the world. It was used as early as the Sixth Century B.C. Sugar beets are the reason that sugar became so affordable. Grown from Australia to Mexico they made it possible to manufacture sugar in significant quantities. Before sugar, honey was used to sweeten everything. Columbus brought sugar from the Caribbean Islands and at the time of the Crusades it was considered a spice. Earlier in history it was regarded as a luxury that the common man could not afford.

We've started mixing our brownies with the main ingredients we need. It takes a pinch of salt to help complete this recipe. Salt was used as money and like sugar was not available to the general public. It's mined throughout the world and extracted from the sea. It's used to cure meat, season food and in this case become a main part of our recipe.

Then we have grains from around the world that we use to make flour. There is rice, corn and wheat flour as well as many others. By taking grain and milling it to a fine powder we can use it to make bread, cookies and of course our brownies.

Then you add baking powder which is a weak acid mixture that leavens our brownies.

Before I go any further I admit that I have a weakness. My name is Red Devine and I am an addict. It's been four days since I had my last brownie. When I see someone combining butter, salt, sugar and cocoa I can't help myself. As the air fills with that amazing chocolate aroma I find myself helpless to its power.

I then would search out vanilla ice cream, fudge and whipping cream without even thinking about it. I am powerless to its effects. I have committed brownies in my heart.

To try and help my addiction I am seeking professional help from these soft brown squares of moist delight and believe that a higher power can help me find my way. I love brownies.

Science and religion have been at odds since the beginning of time. The stars, planets, black holes, dark matter even trees and waterfalls make sense to me. I can even understand the Big Bang theory. But it's almost beyond belief that somehow our planet landed in the exact position it did to sustain life one degree this way we freeze, a degree in the opposite position we fry. What a throw of the dice.

But what about computers, smart phones, the food we eat, the air we breathe. Smart TV's, sky scrapers, planes that fly and cars that drive and the fuel needed to make them head down the road. What about all of that.

If Pharaoh would have known where to dig they could have had "Egypt's Got Talent" during his reign. The actual math to calculate the chances of these things happening cannot be calculated by the most powerful computers that we have today.

Scientist have a more powerful faith than most Christians.

For them to believe that all this just happened is like believing that there has been a man living on the moon making cheese forever.

It takes more faith to believe that our universe just happened than to believe someone else was dealing the cards.

I have a general knowledge of how scientist have proposed that our universe came to be. But here is my main question *"Why are there brownies?"* Why do we have the ingredients to make them? Did chocolate come here by way of a meteorite? Did an alien drop by and leave the Orchid plant we need to produce vanilla? When you think about it brownies take the cake.

We need air to breathe, water to sustain life and without the sun we would be a ball of ice floating in space. There are things we need to stay alive its either an amazing coincidence or a brilliant plan.

But we don't "NEED" brownies of course most of us don't. If I don't eat at least one brownie a month I need to see a doctor. It's called "browniegeness" I will soon launch an effort to raise money, for the needed cure. Will have brown ribbons…

Brownies are a miracle. Made correctly with nuts, vanilla ice cream and hot fudge heaven's not far away. My only conclusion is that brownies are a gift from God. He's that good to us.

I have questioned my faith just like anyone who chooses to serve God. Things happen that can make us question our commitment and our basic beliefs. It's brownies that finally settled my belief in God. There had to be someone, somewhere who put them together.

God knew that you would face troubles and trails. He was aware that there would be tough days, weeks and months. Sometimes there's relationship problems, financial troubles. So, He made brownies. Even though life can be hard, brownies are soft and can soften the blow.

This world is full of beautiful crazy things. Roses that smell beautiful, the soothing sound of the ocean as it wanders to the shore. Magnificent birds, loyal dogs and cats that live and own our homes. It's hard to believe that there wasn't a plan. Someone at the controls.

Once I realized how improbable it was that our planet would have the needed items to make brownies I understood and believed in the providence of God.

To celebrate this new-found faith, I began a quest to learn how to bake brownies myself. Cheesecake brownies, brownies with nuts, brownies made with cookies on top of them. Then I tried brownies made by different companies: Duncan Hines, Ghirardelli, Magic Elves someone had to do the hard work of research. I am glad to report that every brownie I have ate had its good side and from my research there is no greater treat than brownies.

It's the unbelievable fact that brownies exist that helped me secure my deep faith in God. Brownies are my empirical evidence that God exists. After years of in-depth study and research in secret labs and faraway places my conclusion is simple God exists because brownies exist. I continue that same grueling work day by day researching different types of brownies, tasting them, trying every kind I can find. It's one of my callings.

Every time I hear a new revelation about the origins of our universe it confirms what I believe. But it's brownies that prove how detailed our creation is.

He took the time to create a tree in South America, sugar cane and beets. He made sure we had wheat, eggs, and baking powder. And as a beautiful expression of His love an Orchid for vanilla and butter from cows. All of this for those who love brownies it's an amazing expression of how good life can be.

I'm typing on this computer, drive to work in an air-conditioned car and listen to great gospel music along the way. I'm working in a large building full of every comfort I need. On the highway that I drive there are cameras and lights that direct traffic and help keep things safe.

On my way home there are trees, plants and flowers. I breathe in the air that sustains me and reach for water that hydrates me.

It's amazing that the TV I watch grabs shows out of the air and presents them on our screens. My cell phone is connected to almost any person or place on the face of this earth. And what about the bountiful cities and ships on the sea. Consider the food that feeds billions, the fuel to heat our homes and power our vehicles. And bless God for those who use an oven to bake a mess of brownies. It goes without saying that the type of planning that took place to have all these items supporting billions of people daily is beyond belief.

I don't have the kind of faith that says a couple of chemicals bounced together and through some magical event all of this came from that, I just can't see it. Even if it was true someone, somewhere had to push the start button had to have a hand in this, it makes you wonder "*Who lit the fuse?*"

It was God's plan to create, plan and implement the world and universe we live in. Jupiter acts like a great vacuum cleaner removing all kind of debris, asteroids, and meteorites that would have ended our planet eons ago. The fact that the whole system we call our universe had to be placed exactly as it is defies description and practical knowledge.

And what about the bee that little Melipeone Bee. Thank you, God for that. And if He can do all of that then you can believe He can bring your world together "*If you let Him!*" He is the author and finisher of your faith. Honor Him, Praise Him because He cares for you.

Casting all your care upon him; for he careth for you.

1 Peter 5:7

Bonus Science Experiment:

The math is impressive! Here's an experiment you can do at home. There are 100 tiles in each Scrabble game two being blank with the rest being letters. Let's do some science, take the bag full of tiles open it and throw all the tiles on a table at one time. Each time you throw them, look closely at them. Then repeat that same behavior until you create a poem. I hope your wearing comfortable shoes. Random letters thrown in an inexact manner may not even develop one word. Just 100 tiles, our universe is just a little more complicated than that. In fact, you can pass this experiment down to the next generation repeat the experiment and still not get any results.

Let's climb a few trees, build a raft good enough to sail the ocean or spend a morning drinking coffee and watch the sun rise in the east. It's time to laugh, to dance, it's time to be a kid again. Live with renewed hope understand what faith really is and above all reach deep to comprehend how powerful His love really is.

Pass the hot fudge and the ice cream and pecans. Did I ever tell you the story of where ice cream and pecans come from? Well that's another story. I praise God for the brownies!

"Trust in the Lord with all thine heart; and lean not unto thine own understanding.

Proverbs 3:5

"And the peace of God, which passeth all understanding, shall keep your hearts and minds through Christ Jesus."

Philippians 4:7

YOUR 7ᵀᴴ SECRET MISSION

In all things give thanks. Your praise is a confirmation that you have faith in what God's doing in your life. Tough things happen because of what others may have done, victory comes because of what Jesus did.

"Giving thanks always for all things unto God and the Father in the name of our Lord Jesus Christ"

Ephesians 5:20-21

Even if the storm clouds gather, He's right beside you, protecting you. Which brings you to a whole new level of faith. When you try and fix your life without Him you'll pay. Trust Him and your success changes your attitude and raises your altitude. He'll let you stumble if you chose to do so. Hoping you will eventually call Him so He can teach you to walk with confidence.

Life is simple once you learn the right path to take. Life can be hard and extreme. It can be unbearable at times unless you elect to change. It's an election you will win if you take the right approach and direction. Everything is hard before it's easy.

I thought I had to climb tall mountains taking years to find that cave where a wise guru lived. I just needed to find that cave. He would have the answers to life. But on my way to that cave I found an old rugged cross. When I learned the meaning of that cross and who hung there. My existence was transformed. Life became simple and profound.

I found my answers and myself in the pages of the Bible. I will never apologize for where I found them. Through every known problem, concern or life changing event that I've had I found the simple answer to surviving life and thriving in life. Life is simple. God is love.

The world will strip you of every powerful gift you had as a child. The Bible can show you how to hold onto your joy, understand love on a cellular level, As the sun begins to rise you'll be ready for anything coming your way. Don't let your happiness become diluted by the experiences of life.

Never, ever let anyone or anything steal your joy. You may have lived through verbal or physical abuse. As you sat there in your misery you could feel your joy slipping away. Your strength to live fading away like an evening sun setting. It's almost impossible to protect your joy-filled life when it's been stolen. Sometimes we just hand it over to that person or situation that took it. Don't ever let anything or anyone steal your joy.

"The Joy of the Lord is our strength"

What you say makes your day. Speak life change your world instead of it changing you. The things you say and do becomes your roadmap. You and no one else creates the world you live in. It's how you react to life that dictates how you will direct your life. No one else has that type of control of your life.

Power comes when you are grateful, decisions you make are fateful and the road you take will be the path to utter joy or total defeat. Trust Him, love Him, and give Him your life. Then as you learn the secrets of unending joy, go to the kitchen and make up a whole mess of brownies. I'll bring the milk, ice cream and hot fudge.

What an amazing creator we serve.

"I've been accused of still being a kid. I watch the clouds pass by as the wind makes the trees dance and rain causes the flowers to grow. I sing for no reason, jump in the leaves when I have a chance and never miss an opportunity to laugh.

Red Devine

"To speak truly, few adult persons can see nature. Most individuals do not see the sun. At least they have a superficial seeing. The sun illuminates not only the eye of the man but shines into the eye and heart of the child. The lover of nature is he whose inward and outward senses are still truly adjusted to each other; who has retained the spirit of infancy even into the era of manhood." **Ralph Waldo Emerson**

Moment of Mirth: What kind of dog do you get when you mix a pit bull with a laughing hyena? I don't know for sure but when he's laughing you better join in.

TASK #7: Celebrate the third Saturday of the month by declaring it to be the *"Brownies of the month club."* You'll never be closer to God than when you are eating brownies with wonderful, positive people nearby. Once instituted be sure to invite me. **Look for our top five recipes to make brownies on our website reddevine.com**

CHAPTER

8

The Crossroads

One evening in an Indian village, an old Cherokee brave told his grandson about a battle that goes on inside all people.

He said, *"My son, the battle in life is between two wolves inside of us all. One is evil; it's angry, filled with envy, hatred, jealousy, sorrow, regret, greed, arrogance, self-pity, guilt, fear, resentment, inferiority, lies, false pride, superiority and ego. The other is good; encompassed with joy, peace, love, caring, hope, serenity, humility, kindness, benevolence, empathy, generosity, truth, compassion and faith."*

The grandson, trying to grasp what his grandfather had said, thought for a moment and then asked his grandfather *"Which wolf wins?"*

His grandfather the wise old Cherokee, replied, *"The one you feed"*

You have experienced many emotions, trails and problems in life and reacted to them in different ways. You either give in to the issues of life or you dealt with them.

You have chosen different ways to understanding the questions and reasons for life because you have been born to be an adventurer.

You have sought how to fill emptiness, to try to understand who you are, why you are here and what you're supposed to do with your life. Each day brings a brand-new journey of discovery.

It can be challenging to wonder *"Which road do I take?"*

You're at a crossroad: you need to decide which direction you should go north, east, south or west. The direction you take will determine your destiny. This is more than a moment of discovery more than just a destination.

You need a guide someone whose traveled the same road you're on. You need to travel to a place where joy, peace and happiness abide. Life can be challenging for you, living in turmoil, when you have more questions than answers. If life is not working for you, then it's time to take a different road and head in a different direction.

Decisions change your life. As you're standing at the crossroads wondering which road to take you hope you have the right map that leads to the life you've imagined. To live as we did as a kid enjoying every moment of every day.

You may regret your past decisions, which will cripple you from making the right decisions. Remember it's the past that taught you the lessons needed to continue your future. The people you've met, the places you have been the good, the bad and the ugly all of this became enduring lessons that leads you to the right path and direction in life.

Let go of any regrets that you have and learn from your mistakes. Learn from the experiences you've lived through.

Your life is a mirror of the reality you're living. If your financial life has you washing paper plates, or your dog is getting sick of eating month-old Grape Nuts, then it's time to go a different direction and start working towards better days. Your dog would appreciate it.

You have become what you are by every road you've taken, every highway traveled and every mountain you've climbed. It's easy to read the roadmap that shows where you are. And if your journey has not been a happy one, isn't it time to find a new road?

You've may have traveled the wrong roads and paid the price for going there. Your regrets have made you afraid to take any further journeys. Afraid that any new roads might shatter what's left of your life.

Because of this you end up traveling on a never-ending road that circles back to an easy chair of comfort.

Change is the road taken that determines the amount of growth you experience in the future. If there is no growth, then there is no change to the path you're traveling on.

You may be so scared of doing the wrong thing that you're lost trying to do the right thing. What you believe and perceive color your life. Your beliefs can take you down a dead-end road that leads to being boarded in by walls of your own construction. Life is what you make it.

The tongue has the power of life and death, and those who love it will eat of its fruit.

Proverbs 18:21

What you say, you believe. If you speak death then death will eventually come into a relationship, a marriage, a vision or any dreams you may have. It can derail success, and cause failure because the words you speak create the world you travel in.

If you speak life, then a hurting marriage can be saved, a business blossom and new and wonderful adventures can await you.

REDVERB: What you speak becomes what you believe, which becomes what you receive. Changing what you receive happens when you understand what you perceive.

It's the faith you have in your words that creates the life you live. Everyone seeks freedom, joy and love but what you perceive becomes what you believe. If you feel that your life is filled with pain, despair and disappointment and you see no way out you may end up saying "*Why, try!*"

You fall into patterns that are sometimes hard to recognize. These familiar paths become ruts you abide in. A place that seems normal and comfortable. Even the most beautiful dawn can become just another day.

Your perception is everything. It's always about perception

REDVERB: What "YOU" perceive "YOU believe.

No one holds power over you that you do not allow. And nothing will change in your life until you are aware of where you are and where you're going. The power of life and death are on your tongue. If you perceive that life sucks, then it does. Believing there is no hope will certainly make hope disappear.

We can't speak until our minds are engaged and what we say comes directly from what we think.

Very few people stop to think about what they are thinking about. We fly down the highway of life with our specialty coffee, conversing to the world using the technologies we now possess. But we never slow down enough to listen to our own voices. We can connect to anyone, anywhere, at any time, doing whatever. We can share that information with the world.

But we don't use any device program or technology to understand where we're going are what we're becoming. We are alive, but we do not live, we speak but we do not respond, we hear but we do not listen.

To become a kid again we need to understand who we are now and what we want to be.

There is power in negative thinking many people practice it until they have become professionals at the dark side of life.

You have a choice to live a life of positive power or negative energy. Whatever choice you make, I challenge you to give it everything you have. Don't stand in the middle of the road because you can get run over there. This is the crossroads a real turning point in your life. Live a one hundred percent positive life, or dwell continually in the land of the negative it's time to choose.

If your decision is to live a 100% negative life here's some fantastic things to look for and do:

When you drink milk, it should curdle. When you walk into a lighted room the lights should go out. It's a challenge to be one hundred percent negative. You'll need to prepare for any good news coming your way. Life will give you a head start. You may have already internalized many great negative aspects of life. You're on your way. When folks walk on the other side of the road to avoid you, and cats and dogs howl when you pass by. You'll know that you're on your way to making your new goal of depression and despair real.

Here's your guide to living this great new path to the dark side of life. And a few tricks to keep you there. Your goal is that your new negative life will be so compelling, that birds will drop from the sky when you walk by.

The Power of Negative Thinking:

1. **You should always carry a list of negative things-** This helps you invent things that can happen at any given time. When you may feel a little joy, it helps you stay in a negative mood. You could lose your job, get in an accident, lose your hair many great and wonderful things can go wrong. When things seem to be going your way pull out this list and mediate on it. This is a great tool for staying on the dark side of the street.

2. **Develop stress it's your friend-** It's an excellent way to destroy your health. This makes it impossible to sleep. It's an incredible benefit to staying gray all day. If done correctly you'll reach your best goal of total failure in a short period of time.

3. **Create a scenario for your next day:** Learn to make a lifetime opportunity into a complete disaster this helps you build regret for the future. Regret helps you review daily the disaster that happen *"How could I have done that? How stupid am I? I will never get ahead!"*

The Scenario that brings failure! Practice, practice, practice!

You have a job interview tomorrow if you don't get it you won't be able to pay the rent. Your job interview is at 8 a.m. You set your alarm for 7:55 a.m. don't take a shower or do the laundry. Leave your cell phone on and don't charge it. This is a powerful path to negative thinking and is a great tool to use when success may happen!

The night before the interview drive your car until the gas gauge reads "E" for empty. Make sure your clothes are dirty. Leave a message with the interviewers that you'll bring doughnuts. **Remember your goal:** We want 100 percent smile stopping, bad joke telling, nervous energy total and complete absolute negativity.

You've set the stage. Your alarm goes off, *"Oh, no!"* you need to be downtown by 8:00 a.m.! You don't have time to take a shower and all your clothes are dirty! But your intrepid and don't give up easily. You put on some old clothes from the back of the closet, they barely fit. You run out to the car, a button pops on your tight shirt. You start it up and drive a few blocks. *"Now What!"* Yes, you've run out of gas, but you still try and make it to the nearest gas station. You push it five blocks but then you run out of gas.

You call the nearest tow service and realize that you hadn't charged your phone there's not enough power to call the folks waiting to interview you. The tow service shows up and charges you the last bit of money you have left.

As he drives away somethings wrong because you see sparks flying, you yell at him, but he can't hear you as he drives onto the freeway. Trying a last-ditch effort, you call your cousin Cletus. Hoping for a ride to your interview. But no one is home. The message says *"Sorry, but Cletus is in the mountains tending the moonshine call back in a month."* You wonder *"What else can go wrong?"* as your cell phone tries desperately to hold on.. Can you feel the negativity, isn't it great!

Make sure any plan you put into place causes you to not *"Smile for a while"* That you'll experience a powerful, beautiful un-ending day full of negative heart stopping energy.

As you look at your dying phone you see the message, *"Where are you?"* but your phone has now used up all its power. "And where are the doughnuts?" You've lost the chance for that $100,00 a year job with the free home. Then it rains.

Headed back home you're hoping they haven't kicked you out yet. Walking down the street a mad dog comes from across the road and bites your leg. You survive with your life but now you're walking with a limp. Isn't this great! Your doing wonderful meeting your goals.

Now it's there, the rage builds up, stress comes at you like a run-away freight train. Your close to wanting to just cash it all in. You're now living the low life, cynical to the core this is really living!

Somehow through the rain and the pain you get home, and there it is on the door pay the rent or pack up. You open the door drenched, unshaven and wearing clothes that don't fit you slump into the nearest chair. You begin to charge up your phone, it rings. *"Hello, is this the owner of the 93 Dodge Dart in our parking lot?"*

"Yes" you answer *"Why?" It looks like the tow driver who brought your car here used your credit card to go to the Virgin Islands, did you authorize that?"* You're now having an out of body experience. *"Oh, as a friendly reminder your car payment is due, thanks for banking with us!"*

You've got blood on your now torn jeans and your shirt is only halfway on. You reach down to eat the last piece of food in your apartment. bringing this cold hard food to your lips, grease oozes out and lands on the only clean shirt you had. What a glorious day for the power of negative thinking! Your friends will give you a new nick name *"Dr. Death."*

To insure there is no hope it's time to put the last brick in the wall. It's time to worry. You take out that negative list from your now dirty shirt pocket enabling this great gift of worry. It's putting you on the path of utter failure. Wow, this is great.

Worry can be magical. As it kicks in you can envision plagues, floods, fire, earthquakes and destruction. Every conceivable natural disaster known to man. You can worry about things that haven't even happened yet. And once you include worry with your imagination it will become the greatest gift any negative person can ever hope for.

Lower than a whale on the bottom of the ocean who had dug a hole to sleep in, you've taken the negative lifestyle to a whole new level!

The only peace you have is the piece of your car still sitting at the bank. You're mastering the dark side of life!

There is an old Indian saying, *"If you have one foot on the shore and the other in the canoe you're going to get wet"* I respect the individual who leaves nothing behind. A person with the commitment to follow through one hundred percent (Barring anything illegal, immoral or harmful to others) I may not agree with your choices or share your beliefs, but I do honor a total commitment to your goals.

Living a double life creates failure on so many levels. Happy for the moment and downbeat the next. It's a tiring way to live. As kids we spent too much time playing to spend much time worrying about tomorrow. It's time to become a kid again.

Here's a normal everyday discussion you may hear sitting at lunch with your friends *"Hey, did I tell you that I got bit by a black widow spider!"* *"The pain was terrible, just look at my arm!"*

The next person at the table says *"That's tough, but you think that's bad. I fell off a ladder and broke my ankle, I wish I had been bit by a spider!"*

Not to be outdone your next friend pipes in, *"Yeah that's got to hurt, I forgot to tell you guys about my car wreck! I slammed into a wall trying to miss a dog on the road. My neck was twisted like a tornado. The doctor says it won't be long and I probably won't be able to walk!"*

Now prouder than most your fourth friend speaks up *"I don't know how you stand it. But dude, did you know that I was riding the city bus last week when it careened off the road and hit a gas truck! The accident was so terrible that people died! They rushed me to the hospital and took me to the emergency room. In their haste to fix everyone they accidently put my left foot on my right leg and my right foot on my left leg! I almost died three times on the operating table. And I lost a lot of blood. But because of the mix up with my feet, when I walk I walk in circles!"*

Everyone is silent for a moment and they look at each other. They say *"Wow, man you win that's the worst thing we've ever heard!"*

He throws his fist in the air with a look of joy. *"Yes, I have the worst problem in the room!"* As everyone gives him a standing ovation.

Somethings wrong with this picture. People are proud of their problems. They want to talk about them, share them with anyone that will listen. *"Look at my problem, isn't it great? Don't you wish you had problems like me?"* We show pictures of our problems, pet them, parade them, and carry them around like badges of honor.

I hope you want to be different, you want to get back to a place where life is fun. You're going to make a pledge from this day forward to live a one hundred percent positive life. If you do you're on the road to recovering that child-like spirit.

Speak Life.

Let's look at that last scenario but change it up a bit.

Same room, different people.

"Hey, did I tell you guys that when I washed my clothes I found a twenty dollar bill I had forgotten about? I really needed the money. Cool, Huh!

The person beside him says *"That's cool. But did you guys know that I have been married to Bertha for fifteen years, right? Well after fifteen years my wife said something to me that shocked me. Are you guys sitting down? She said I was RIGHT! My wife actually said I was right! "*

At this moment each man took off his hat and put their hand near their heart. Their mouths wide open in disbelief. They tried to collect themselves. One of them looked at his friend and said *"Wow, that's never happened to me. What did it feel like?* He answered, *"I really don't know, it hasn't sunk in yet."*

Trying hard to collect himself the friend next to him patted him on the shoulder. *"I will never forget this moment! I woke up this morning feeling fantastic, I realized I had another beautiful day to live. Recently I learned to cast my cares on God and my life has changed dramatically!*

Your boss was standing close by and heard the conversations. The room was charged with positive vibes. The only answer he could come up with is to call Human Resources because these guys must be on something!

My point is simple: No more riding the fence-it's all or nothing. The dark side can be deadly, standing in the light is the only way to see a brighter future. Let's work on being sold out to becoming the most powerful. Positive people in the world.

The reality of this situation is to give yourself permission to change. I can't change you, the pope can't change you, Billy Graham and

Sister Theresa could come over to your house and beg you to change. But nothing changes until you're ready to change.

If you believe that there is no hope left in the world, you're right. But if you believe the world is full of hope, faith and love and it's available to everyone, then you are also right. Henry Ford said, *"If you believe you can or you believe you can't you're right."*

It's your personal beliefs that guide you, hide you but they will always sit beside you. They will either make you sail high or sink as low as you can go.

You need to take inventory of what you're thinking once you do you'll understand where you are and where you need to go to get there. Your actions, guided by your words will create the basis for the life you live.

Speak life.

You're at the crossroads. It's time to make the ultimate decision about who you want to become. Walk away from the past, live for today and pray for a fantastic future.

Stop for a moment take a deep breath and see what you've become. You can see a clear direction to the right road that takes you where you want to be.

If you are experiencing a broken heart it won't show up on an MRI or X-RAY. You can heal from a broken leg, it's a broken heart that keeps you from having a better life. You always see the world through your heart's pain or it's joy.

As kids we believed we could fight one hundred ninjas' at once. Jump over a fifty-foot wall in one leap.

And walk on rice paper without leaving a tear. We never saw an obstacle we could not overcome.

It's called "**Solution Based Thinking**"

REDVERB: There are no such things as problems just solutions.

Problems are everywhere, some life-changing others barely noticeable. Every problem you have has a solution. Some seem insurmountable, your mind reels, your hands sweat. Your heart beats wildly as you wrap your mind around it.

Every solution to these problems start with one action. The first step. You've learned to let go of your past, how powerful your imaginations can be and now you've made the quality decision to live a one hundred percent positive life style.

Few people understand what motivates them. Why you do or say the things you do? In the heat of an argument a lifetime of problems, situations, heart break comes out of nowhere. It's a collection of all those things that you've never dealt with.

We are all human; your neighbors are just like you. You've had great moments of joy and days when the tears flowed. Your pastor, sorry to let you know has had his up and down moments in life. We all make mistakes and do things that we regret later. There is not one person on the face of this earth that has not been in a self-induced quandary.

Make mistakes, learn from the experience, do them only once. Then you'll know how to walk away from any situation like you just plowed through. Mistakes mean you are trying, you're willing to grow.

This allows you to become aware of your weaknesses. Don't focus on your strengths; they are there to support you. Focus on eliminating your weaknesses. By honestly looking where you're at you'll be able to map out where you want to go.

Write down every thought, keep a journal that will revel your innermost conversations. Your self-talk becomes your feelings which becomes your life. When you speak you're bringing life or death to your future. Writing down what you feel will help cure any self-defeating, heart-stopping, stinking thinking that you might have. **"Don't wait...DO IT NOW!**

Casting down imaginations, and every high thing that exalts itself against the knowledge of God and bringing into captivity every thought to the obedience of Christ.

2 Corinthians 10:5

Every problem your facing has a solution

If there is was a fence in the way kids will find a loose board to go through.

Look at the problem no matter how great and ask yourself. *"What's the first step I need to take to solve this?"* Addiction, a marriage in trouble where do you go to get the help you need.

Understand that none of us have all the tools we need to solve everything. If you want to build a house, you'll need a carpenter that knows what tools he needs for the job and how to use them.

He has the understanding and tools he needs to build it. But when it comes to doing the electrical he'll have to hire a sub-contractor to help him. Because a carpenter has no idea how to use the tools needed to do that part of the job.

Sometimes you need someone to help you a pastor, a counselor, a friend someone who has the tools to show you the way out of the trap you find yourself in. When someone comes to me with a problem my first question is *"Have you developed a plan that will help you find the solution to your problem?"*

When you take the first step and need my help you first need to develop your own solution and share it with me. We may not be able to use the solution you've come up with. But at least I know that you're on the right track willing to find the answer you need. Together we can work on it and find that fix needed to destroy any problem you have.

As you focus on solutions instead of problems you begin to feel in control of that runaway train you call life. Solution-based thinking causes your brain to immediately start hatching out a plan to eliminate the problem you face. A positive lifestyle begins to emerge as you see the problems in your life melt away. That success emboldens you to take on even more. Because success breeds success. Commit to change.

When you walk down the street dogs will want to be near you, doves will fly by you. Streetlights will light up even in the daytime. And the people you meet will become changed by the power of the positive vibes that surround you. You can do this, your world can change, joy will multiply, and hope will fire up your faith. And even if your car payment is due, you'll start working on the solution to pay it laughing all the way to the bank.

REDVERB: Lives change when someone listens and has a kind word, a simple hug or a word of encouragement. The simplest act of love can turn a life around.

When it seems that hope is lost, and success is far away. Hold tight to your dreams you may be only two steps away from your miracle.

Red Devine

1970-Taking Inventory

It was a beautiful Northern California afternoon; It was the summer of love, things were changing all around us. Everyone was hurrying to get to their classes it was a cacophony of laughter and confusion as people talked as they walked.

Lockers opening and closing added to the din with their loud metallic clanging. Some were getting books and others putting notes in from their last class. I walked through the crowd despondent I had failed a test I should have passed easily. Things at home were not going well and it was taking its toll.

I recited my personal mantra *"I'm stupid and I will never make it."* I walked head down dwelling on the fact that I had failed.

Out of nowhere a scripture I had read the day before came to me *"For though we live in the world, we do not wage war as the world does. The weapons we fight with are not the weapons of this world. On the contrary, they have divine power to demolish strongholds."*

"Divine power, divine power," I could use a little of that. the devil had a few strongholds in my life, I had been a Christian for a very short time. I opened my locker *"No weapon formed against me will prosper"* God was talking to me and the scriptures were flowing. Divine power, no weapon, pulling down strongholds this was all well and good but *"how?"* Was there a way to *"demolish"* strongholds?

I was at war with satan since the day I had watched him steal my nickel. He was trying every way he could to defeat me. I knew that he lived in the shadows where no one could see him. I had fallen prey to the devil's arguments and suggestions. And I was looking to any advantage to overcome what he was trying to build in my life. To beat him at his own game.

I closed my locker heading to class the hallways were still filled with everyone scurrying around. Suddenly, I stopped in my tracks, the last clue to the puzzle hit me like a brick.

Good old 2 Corinthians *"Casting down imaginations, and every high thing that exalteth itself against the knowledge of God and bringing into captivity "**Every thought"** to the obedience of Christ."* And then again *"The weapons of our warfare are not carnal, but **MIGHTY through God to the pulling down of strongholds."***

Every thought! My life had been filled with a series of up and down emotions fueled by the feeling of being unloved, discarded and abused. These scriptures kept circling in my mind like an eight-track tape (eight track tapes were once cool, look it up on Google)" **You're an idiot and you'll never make it."**

I dropped my books and sat down leaning against the wall, as folks passed by me I wondered if anyone else had fought this battle.

I thought about what I had been thinking about for the first time in my life.

Over and over this thought played through my mind it was a never-ending loop of destruction and personal defeat ingrained in my soul. *"I'm stupid and I will never make it."* It was a revelation; it was earth shattering to be aware of this stronghold that was so disabling. Until that exact moment I wasn't aware that it had been there for years.

That thought had been buried deep in my soul from somewhere in my past and the sad thing was I'd believed it.

I became instantly agitated by the fact that I'd said it and believed it. For the first time in my life I took control over this one thought. I stood up and started pacing back and forth like an expectant father waiting for a child to be born. Except my child was a new revelation.

"I am not stupid, and I will make it" I said in a timid voice. Something was bursting inside of me as many years of frustration and defeat became trampled by this amazing truth. My old enemy had tried desperately to not only steer me back to the dark side but keep me there.

Now I was mad. I said louder this time with more feeling *"I AM NOT STUPID, AND I WILL MAKE IT!"* Everyone in the hallway started looking at me and walked as far away from me as they could. I looked around to make sure no one had called security. I began to cry as I felt the chains begin to drop. I now paced faster looking for those guys in the white suits carrying a net.

But the shackles had fallen now, a new freedom was blossoming. I could hear that rusty iron lock break in two, making an echoing sound I will never forget. As it fell my heart beat faster and my lungs filled with air, everyone was looking now wondering if I had lost my mind. I yelled **"I AM NOT STUPID, AND I WILL MAKE IT!"**

This time everyone heard me loud and clear I was sure the principal wasn't that far behind. It was time for me to get to class.

I had taken a thought captive for the first time in my life. Reality set in. It's time to get in control of my life instead of it controlling me. All the negative, crippling thoughts that was in my mish-mosh of a brain came to me in a moment in time. I began writing a new subtext to my life. Freeing my mind to become a powerful weapon against the strongholds that held me captive for so long.

A light flooded through this new open door. I stopped before reaching my class frantically starting to write down the flood of negativity I had lived in. They came fast and furious I now understood how to dig my way out of this dark hole I had been buried in.

It was time to retrain my brain and restrain from pain. I wrote down every thought and kept a journal. It's the things in life that get you. You become affected by everything, when nothing goes right. At times frustrated, it seems there isn't anything you can do about it. Those thoughts and many others had been stored in my mind. I was in a battle for my mind and soul and I had just loaded up a new weapon the devil could not fight.

The Bible is the greatest self-help book ever written. It has the simple secrets of how to live an amazing powerful life. As every day goes by, you get stronger and wiser by understanding it's truths and examining its secrets. Eventually all the things that trouble you no longer have power over you. **Below is a list of some powerful weapons you can use:**

"Nay in all these things we are more than conquerors through Him that loved us."

Romans 8:37

"Though I speak with the tongues of men and angels and have not love, I am become as a sounding brass or a tinkling cymbal. And though I have the gift of prophecy, and understand all mysteries, and all knowledge; and though I have all faith, so that I could move mountains, and have not love, I am nothing. And though I bestow all my goods to feed the poor, and though I give my body to be burned, and have not love, it profiteth me nothing. Love suffereth long and is kind; love envieth

not; love vaunteth not itself, is not puffed up, Doth not behave itself unseemly, seeketh not her own, is not easily provoked, thinketh no evil, Rejoiceth not in iniquity, but rejoiceth in the truth; Beareth all things, beleiveth all things, hopeth all things, endureth all things.

1 Corinthians 13:1-7

"And we know that all things work together for good to them that love God, to them who are the called according to His purpose"

Romans 8:28

Therefore, if any man be in Christ, he is a new creature; old things are passed away; behold things have become new.

2 Corinthians 5:17

"Giving thanks always for all things unto God and the Father in the name of our Lord Jesus."

Ephesians 5:20-21

"I can do all things through Christ which strengtheneth me"

2 Timothy 2:7

"My little children, let us love in word, neither in tongue; but in deed, and in truth. And hereby we know that we are of the truth and shall assure our hearts before Him. For if our heart condemns us, God is greater than our heart and knoweth all things. Beloved, if our heart condemns us not, then we have confidence toward God; And whatsoever we ask, we receive of Him, because we keep his commandments and do those things that are pleasing in His sight.

1 John 3:18-22

"And God shall wipe away all tears from their eyes; and there shall there be no more death, neither sorrow, nor crying, neither shall there be any more pain: for the former things are passed away.

Revelation 21

"No weapon that is formed against thee shall prosper; and every tongue that shall rise against thee in judgement thou shall condemn. This is the heritage of the servants of the Lord"

Isaiah 54:17

"Which of you by taking thought can add one cubit unto his stature? And why take ye thought for raiment? Consider the lilies of the field, how they grow; they toil not, neither do they spin: And yet I say unto you, that Solomon in all his glory was not arrayed like one of these. Wherefore, if God so clothe the grass of the field, which today is, and tomorrow is cast into the oven, shall He not much more clothe you, O ye of little faith? Therefore, take no thought, saying, what shall we eat? Or, what shall we drink? or, Wherewithal shall we be clothed? (For after all these things do the Gentiles seek) for your heavenly Father knoweth that ye have need of all these things. But seek ye first the kingdom of God, and His righteousness; and all these things shall be added unto you. Take therefore no thought for the morrow: for the morrow shall take thought for the things of itself. Sufficient unto the day is the evil thereof.

Matthew 6:27-34

He giveth power to the faint; and to them that have no might he increaseth strength.

Isaiah 40:29

Fear thou not; for I am with thee: be not dismayed; for I am thy God: I will strengthen thee; yea, I will help thee; yea, I will uphold thee with the right hand of my righteousness.

Isaiah 41:10

If any of you lack wisdom, let him ask of God, that giveth to all men liberally, and upbraideth not; and it shall be given him.

James 1:5

Therefore, I say unto you, what things soever ye desire, when ye pray, believe that ye receive them, and ye shall have them.

Mark 11:24

But my God shall supply all your need according to his riches in glory by Christ Jesus.

Philippians 4:19

Be careful for nothing; but in everything by prayer and supplication with thanksgiving let your requests be made known unto God. And the peace of God, which passeth all understanding, shall keep your hearts and minds through Christ Jesus.

Philippians 4:6-7

Focusing on these promises and the hundreds of others breaks the chains around your heart. The chains that bound up your joy, captured your peace and enslaved your love, even your ability to feel.

Understanding these truths eliminates your limitations and sets you free. Your family, your friends can't limit you, the abuse you suffered no longer matters. Nothing can limit you from becoming what you've dreamed to be. There is only one thing that can limit you and define you and **that's you!**

If you let others limit you then that's your problem, not theirs. Don't let anyone, anything, or anywhere limit or define you again. You can exist with a broken heart but it's hard to live with its effects. You see the world through its pain and the emotional turmoil. Take inventory, write every day in your journal. God loves you just the way you are. It's time to be free.

YOUR 8ᵀᴴ SECRET MISSION

1. Discern the negative but promote the positive

2. Your mind is the battleground of all significant victories or debilitating defeats.

3. Take inventory- write in you journal daily, review weekly

4. Follow your plan

5. Determine that from now on its 100% or nothing

6. Eat Brownies

7. Never limit yourself...be willing to change and rearrange

To enable the best of life, move forward with the rest of your life. To step higher, see brighter, love deeper, care more. This day, this hour, this minute, this second is the time to make the right choice. The choice to emotional stability and harmony begins when you grasp them, hold them and keep them as your own.

Wait for nothing, let no one dissuade you or keep you from this mission of finding your place in the sun. To experience a new dawn with unimaginable possibilities. Finding that place you've been looking for.

The choice is yours and yours alone make it a good one and make it now. Life "can and will" change if you let it. Take a moment and imagine this new world where you finally control life and you've found once again the heart of a child. Full of faith believing that anything is possible.

Pessimism Leads to weakness, optimism to power **William James**

Weakness is caused by a lack of faith and the constant belief that hope does not exist. **Red Devine**

Moment of Mirth: A burglar breaks into a house. He starts shining his light around looking for valuables. Some nice things catch his eye, and as he reaches for them, he hears, "Jesus is watching you." Startled, the burglar looks for the speaker. Seeing no one, he keeps putting things in his bag, again, he hears, "Jesus is watching you." This time, he sees a parrot. "Who are you?" the burglar asks. "Moses," the bird replied. "Who the heck would name a bird Moses?" the man laughed. "I dunno," Moses answered, "I guess the same kind of people that would name a hundred-pound foaming at the mouth crazy Rottweiler Jesus."

"Finally, brethren, whatsoever things are true, whatsoever things are honest, whatsoever things are just, whatsoever things are pure, Whatsoever things are lovely, whatsoever things of good report; if there be any virtue, if there be any praise, think on these things.

Philippians 4:8

Task #8: Buy a bag of marbles and learn to play with a friend!

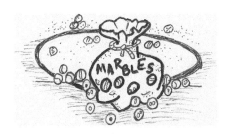

CHAPTER

Green Beans and Threshing Machines

Y ou born to dream, made in the image of God, hard wired to create. It doesn't matter if you believe in God or not. You're a creator.

"The only way to predict your future is to create it."

What type of world are you creating?

Creating life starts with a seed. When a seed is properly planted and cared for it can becomes the life-saving plant that you need. God had a vision and that vision became the seed that created our universe and the world we live in.

This complicated place we call earth.

And God said, Let the earth bring forth grass, the herb yielding seed, and the fruit tree yielding fruit after his kind, whose seed Is, in itself, upon the earth: and it was so. And the earth brought forth grass, and herb yielding seed after his kind, and the tree yielding fruit, whose seed was, in itself, after his kind: and God saw that it was good.

Genesis 1:11-12

Life must be created. Someone must plant the seed. The same creator who plants the seed must know what, why and where to plant it. Understanding once the seed is planted life will begin.

And God said, let us make man in our image, after our likeness: and let them have dominion over the fish of the sea, and over the fowl of the air, and over the cattle, and over all the earth, and over every creeping thing that creepeth upon the earth. So, **God created man in his own image, in the image of God created he him; male and female created he them***. And God blessed them, and God said unto them, be fruitful, and multiply, and replenish the earth, and subdue it: and have dominion over the fish of the sea, and over the fowl of the air, and over every living thing that moveth upon the earth. And God said, Behold, I have given you every herb bearing seed, which is upon the face of all the earth, and every tree, in the which is the fruit of a tree yielding seed; to you it shall be for meat. And to every beast of the earth, and to every fowl of the air, and to everything that creepeth upon the earth, wherein there is life, I have given every green herb for meat: and it was so.*

Genesis 1:26-30

Our creator put everything we need to live in place. Planned everything in the most minute detail. And then created his best work. Man and woman.

He created them in His image.

im·age synonyms: reflection, mirror image, likeness conception, impression, idea, perception, notion; "**he's the image of his father**" synonyms: double, **living image**, look-alike, **clone, copy, twin,**

duplicate, **exact likeness**, **mirror image**, doppelgänger; "**we are made in the image of God**"

Clone, duplicate, exact likeness, made in the image of God. You were born to be like Him. A visionary, a dreamer, a creator.

Creation begins when the seed is planted. When you tend a plant, and fertilize it, it becomes a greater version of itself. Once the seed is planted creation has begun. You can't change what you've created because that is the past tense of creation. Creation is the beginning and once started it takes on a life of its own. Whatever you've created is building your future. Be careful what you plant.

Always look at the outside of the seed package because what you plant will become who and what you are.

If you sow hate, then hatred will follow you. If you steal you will be stolen from, that seed will produce an abundance of lost possessions, lost faith, and can steal everything you own are care for.

If you plant corn you get corn. You can meditate for weeks, fast and pray even wish that you could grow a crop of green beans. But once you plant corn no matter what you do it becomes corn.

He that hath no rule over his own spirit is like a city that is broken down, and without walls.

Proverbs 25:28

Controlling your destiny means controlling your creation, the direction of your life is created by the decisions you make. Don't let satan rule your spirit. He'll create walls that are hard to break down.

*Be not deceived; God is not mocked: **for whatever a man soweth, that shall he reap.***

Galatians 6:7

Whatever you plant determines your crop. That's not some crazy religious teaching, it's a fact, Jack. Some call it Karma, some justice but it's all the same.

Understanding the truth, a seed represents a new beginning, a new life. Find a good piece of ground to plant in and you'll be rewarded by your efforts.

Let's make the rest of your life the best of your life.

What will you create? What will you plant. If you plant love, love multiplies. If you give, then you will be given to. There are very few guarantees in life but this I guarantee *"Whatsoever you soweth you will reap."* No matter what you've planted in the past your future is determined by what you plant now.

If the crop you've planted has brought pain, depression even despair. It's time to plow the ground under and plant again.

Creation *"God's gift to you"* is the starting point. You were born in a physical world full of murder, mayhem and death. Just watch the news for an hour or so. You can see that some have planted some very destructive crops. In fact, your life has been affected by your family tree a result of what your family planted long ago.

But there's good news each day you live there's a new adventure awaiting you. Stay open to new vistas and remain teachable this will keep what you create fresh and new. A child-like curiosity is what causes life to blossom and good crops to grow.

That is why we never give up, though our bodies are dying, our spirits are being renewed every day.

2 Corinthians 4:16

He healeth the broken in heart, and bindeth up their wounds.

Psalms 147:3

You're free to accomplish anything you want in life. And its power is evident. Your plan includes understanding your present. And then evaluate where you want to be. A good farmer plans, choses the right seed and the best ground to plant in to receive the maximum potential. This brings him the best profit.

Then he prays for rain. There's not a farmer on earth that doesn't depend on the weather for a good crop. There are things a farmer can't control so he must have faith and trust that God will do His part.

God put into place certain rules to live by because He's a good father. The only reason those rules exist is to give you the guidelines you need to live an awesome life. If you listen and act accordingly your crop will grow multiplying beyond what you ever expected.

Jesus said, *"Be of good cheer, for I have overcome the world."* He was crucified died and buried and then rose again. When He did He took the world back from satan. In the beginning the devil tricked Adam and Eve into giving up paradise their decision gave satan dominion over the earth. That's the first bad seed that was planted. What Jesus did was give us the ability to re-sign the lease that the devil stole, on an individual basis. When you ask Jesus into your life you once again have dominion over the earth through Him.

That decision gives you the power and authority over any seed that satan has planted or will plant. Giving yourself to God insures your crop will flourish. But all God's promises are conditional. If you try to go it alone, you will receive a bad crop. With God you will learn what to plant and where to plant. And then *"The rain will come"*

The devil puts you in bondage where freedom cannot ring. That's why God gave use the best *"User's Manual"* available "The Bible" Study it, understand it, it's the best guide any farmer can have.

Humans produce human life. The Holy Spirit creates spiritual life. It doesn't matter what church you go to, it doesn't matter if you kneel or stand when you pray. All God wants is a real relationship with you. A transforming, renewing awe-inspiring relationship where He can teach you all the secrets of an overcoming life.

Being born-again is the best way to becoming a kid again. Reborn into a family of powerful saints working their way to the Father. As a kid again, there will be times when you'll fail but learn from that failure. As you learn you become more than the devil can handle. Remember you immediately enter the Kingdom of God; the Kingdom of God is within you. It's like taking an 880-volt electric line and charging your batteries for ever. Your tapping into God's resources.

We're not talking about church doctrine or some religious rules. We're talking about Biblical principles. Paul said in Romans:

"For as many as are led by the Spirit of God, they are the sons of God."

Romans 8:1

The power of the life- giving spirit has freed you from the life-taking power of satan.

"If you confess with your mouth that Jesus is Lord and believe in your heart that God raised Him from the dead, you will be saved."

Romans 8:6

Saved from the pain, depression, hate, and the fear of a very dark world. Powered by the revealing Light of God. You begin a new journey, a new hope a brand-new life, you're His children. He loves you and cares for you under His wing.

Then they cried unto the Lord in their trouble, and he saved them out of their distresses. He brought them out of darkness and the shadow of death and brake their bands in sunder. Oh, that men would praise the Lord for his goodness, and for his wonderful works to the children of men! For he hath broken the gates of brass and cut the bars of iron in sunder.

Psalm 107:13-16

At times I was brilliant then at other times stupid as a rock. But I've learned to let go and let God His love has overtaken my life and rearranged my fighting style. Now with Super Ninja spiritual moves that confuse satan. Every day there is a calm, solid, amazing love guiding me it changes me every moment that I breathe. Joy has become an amazing foundation to my life. Unmovable, unstoppable joy.

The only way to limit God from giving you total freedom, jubilant joy and a present peace is to limit His influence in your life. Give Him something and He will give you everything. Plant the right seed in good ground.

A farmer plants seeds to grow fruit, that's where his profits come from. It's what he is supported by. What you seek is the Fruit of the Spirit. It's what you gain by planting, tending and understanding how to harvest the crop you've given to God.

In Galatians the fifth Chapter the rewards for your efforts is spelled out. This is a progressive list. You cannot have the whole list until you start with love. It's the starting point for gaining and receiving the whole life-changing *"Fruit of the Spirit."*

But the fruit of the Spirit is love, **(then)** *joy,* **(then)** *peace,* **(after that)** *longsuffering,* **(then you receive)** *gentleness,* **(and)** *goodness,* **(which then establishes)** *faith,* **(and)** *Meekness,* **(And finally)** *temperance: against such there is no law.*

Galatians 5:22-23

The Fruit of the Spirit is love. The most powerful mis-understood force in the universe. The Bible tells us that *"God is Love"* Accepting God's love is the moment you become invaded by its power. For the first time in your life you experience real love. Unstoppable, unbelievable, unchanging, unrelenting, love.

It's the fruit of the spirit.

When you understand its power, undeniable changes happen in your behavior. You need to understand that it's a progressive list you can't have real joy until you first experience God's fantastic love. Peace, faith and temperance become a part of you as you reach each level gained by understanding the fruit of the spirit. Falling in love fills you with joy and peace which becomes a part of your new character. When you have real love, joy, and peace it's easy to be longsuffering or patient. With these new gifts you understand the power of gentleness and goodness no longer used and abused. Your heart of stone becomes tender. You're experiencing the first effects of the *"**Fruit of The Spirit.**"*

After these have completed their work in your life along comes faith and meekness.

My children knew I loved them, and knew I would never hurt them, they knew that they would always be taken care of, when I held them they knew I would never let them go. God will always be there for you as you seek Him. Faith grows when it is planted in love, joy and peace.

When love has overtaken you, you'll never stray from that love, that peace and that joy. Temperance is staying away from the things that your Father says will hurt you.

There's strength in temperance you remain in a place where the devil cannot reach you. You've gained the secrets of an overcoming life. What you'll gain is the release of pain you've become amazingly sane. You've just won the game. A foundation of eternal love never to be the same.

Love is not an emotion or a feeling it is an unstoppable force. As usual the devil has counterfeited love. A love that has little power to change you. God's love becomes a power source designed to help you through the hardest of times. Because He will never leave you or forsake you.

You've become a new creature a brand-new creation. All these gifts become the center of who you are, and it starts with love. If you love someone really love them, you would never stray from that relationship. These gifts make you that powerful.

Once they become part of you, satan has nothing to do with you. Love binds you to God and Gods spirit emboldens you. And because of this life-changing "*Fruit*" satan has nothing to snare you with. His tricks fall by the wayside they no longer work. But God's grace and mercy are there for the times you may not measure up. The deeper you fall in love with God the more powerful you become, the more "***Gooder***" your life becomes.

For I will pour water upon him that is thirsty, and floods upon the dry ground: I will pour my spirit upon thy seed, and my blessing upon thine offspring

Isaiah 44:3

And I will give them one heart, and I will put a new spirit within you; and I will take the stony heart out of their flesh, and will give them a heart of flesh

Ezekiel 11-19

The Spirit of the Lord is upon me, because he hath anointed me to preach the gospel to the poor; he hath sent me to heal the brokenhearted, to preach deliverance to the captives, and recovering of sight to the blind, to set at liberty them that are bruised

Luke 4:18

Jesus answered, Verily, verily, I say unto thee, except a man be born of water and of the Spirit, he cannot enter into the kingdom of God.

John 3:5

That which is born of the flesh is flesh; and that which is born of the Spirit is spirit.

John 3:6

And it shall come to pass in the last days, saith God, I will pour out of my Spirit upon all flesh: and your sons and your daughters shall prophesy, and your young men shall see visions, and your old men shall dream dreams:

Acts 2:17

For the law of the Spirit of life in Christ Jesus hath made me free from the law of sin and death.

Romans 8:2

For they that are after the flesh do mind the things of the flesh; but they that are after the Spirit the things of the Spirit.

Romans 8:5

For as many as are led by the Spirit of God, they are the sons of God
Romans 8:14

The Spirit itself beareth witness with our spirit, that we are the children of God:

Romans 8:16

Now the Lord is that Spirit: and where the Spirit of the Lord is, there is liberty.

2 Corinthians 3:17

For he that soweth to his flesh shall of the flesh reap corruption; but he that soweth to the Spirit shall of the Spirit reap life everlasting.

Galatians 6:8

For God hath not given us the spirit of fear; but of power, and of love, and of a sound mind.

2 Timothy 1:7

There is therefore now no condemnation to them which are in Christ Jesus, who walk not after the flesh, but after the Spirit. For the law of the Spirit of life in Christ Jesus hath made me free from the law of sin and death. For what the law could not do, in that it was weak through the flesh, God sending his own Son in the likeness of sinful flesh, and for sin, condemned sin in the flesh: That the righteousness of the law might be fulfilled in us, who walk not after the flesh, but after the Spirit. For they that are after the flesh do mind the things of the flesh; but they that are after the Spirit the things of the Spirit. For to be carnally minded is death; but to be spiritually minded is life and peace. And if Christ be in you, the body is dead because of sin; but the Spirit is life because of righteousness. For if ye live after the flesh, ye shall die: but if ye through the Spirit do mortify the deeds of the body, ye shall live. For as many as are led by the Spirit of God, they are the sons of God. The Spirit itself beareth witness with our spirit, that we are the children of God: And if children, then heirs; heirs of God, and joint-heirs with Christ; For I reckon that the sufferings of this present time are not worthy to be compared with the glory which shall be revealed in us. And we know that all things work together for good to them that love God, to them who are the called according to his purpose. What shall we then say to these things? If God be for us, who can be against us? He that spared not his own Son, but delivered him up for us all, how shall he not with him also freely give us all things? Who shall separate us from the love of Christ? shall tribulation, or distress, or persecution, or famine, or nakedness, or peril, or sword? Nay, in all these things we are more than conquerors through him that loved us. For I am persuaded, that neither death, nor life, nor angels, nor principalities, nor powers, nor things present, nor things to come, nor height, nor depth, nor any other creature, shall be able to separate us from the love of God, which is in Christ Jesus our Lord.

(Parts of) Romans 8

YOUR 9ᵀᴴ SECRET MISSION

What you believe…you Receive

1. Plant good seed

2. Allow God to teach you

3. Understand that the *"Fruit"* is your main goal.

4. It's a life-giving Spirit that invades you.

A kid's story:

A little girl's teacher in Sunday school asked what she was making with her Crayola crayons. She said, *"I'm drawing God!"* The teacher said, "But no one knows what God looks like." The little girl said, *"Give me a minute."* Children know what God looks like, they see Him with their heart.

Moment of Mirth:

A man on a Caribbean vacation decides to go horseback riding. He visits a local church that rents horses to ride in the countryside. The local pastor who raised the horses was a very religious man. He explained that all his horses were religious horses. He explained to the visitor that to make the horse go you need to say, *"Praise God!"* And to make the horse stop you need to say "Amen!"

So, he rented the horse with the pastors blessing and as he rode through the village and headed toward the forest he passed a bee hive and suddenly his horse was stung by a bee. In pain and shock the horse bolted and started running in a full gallop. Up ahead the man could see a dangerous high cliff that the horse was headed for. He began to panic the horse was running so fast he was afraid to jump. *"Whoa, Horse!"* he yelled but nothing happened, the cliff was getting closer to that high cliff that dropped to the rocks below. He began to pray as the horse kept running at breakneck speed now only a few yards from the cliff and his certain death. Dear God, save me, he prayed!!! He finished his prayer and at the top of his lungs yelled out *"AMEN!"*

The horse hearing the command stopped just a foot away from the cliff as small rocks and pieces of grass tumbled over the cliff falling to the rocks below. He hung on for dear life his heart racing, he was barely able to breathe. He was careful not to move a muscle.

He then carefully leaned over to look at the cliff with its three-hundred-foot drop to certain death and the jagged rocks below. Wiping away the sweat from his face he caught his breath. He was so relieved that he had survived this near-death experience that he yelled out "PRAISE THE LORD!" The funeral's next Sunday.

"I believe God is managing affairs and that He doesn't need any advice from me. With God in charge, I believe everything will work out for the best in the end. So, what is there to worry about?"

Henry Ford

"It's about the journey mine and yours and the lives we touch, the legacy we leave, and the world we can change for the better."

Coach Dungy

TASK #9: Buy some good seeds, plant them and watch them grow!

CHAPTER

10

The Formula

Time to decide...

The situations in life don't create you. But the decisions you make in those situations dictate what you'll become.

You now possess the secrets to becoming a kid again. Freedom is built on the foundation that guilt has no place in your life. Free of the past, living for the day, releasing those things that stole joy right out of your soul.

In Matthew eighteen the disciples were fighting about who would be the greatest in the kingdom of God someday. Jesus called a small child to Him and said, *"I tell you the truth, unless you turn from your sins and become like little children, you will never get into the kingdom of God."*

They then asked who would be the greatest in Heaven? Jesus said,

"So, anyone who becomes as humble as this little child is the greatest in the Kingdom of Heaven. And anyone who welcomes a little child on my behalf is welcoming me." Jesus lives big in anyone that sees the world as a kid sees the world.

With God your life is not falling apart, it is falling into place. He doesn't want you to give up anything on the contrary he wants to give you everything. But you must follow the right road to get there.

You can live a wonderfully, powerful, incredible, life changing, tremendous faith-filled life. An all- consuming, joyful, peaceful life full of hope and promise. Money, power and fame don't get you there. Drugs or alcohol doesn't get you there. Once you have the *"Kingdom of God"* within you your life becomes a super-fantastic spiritual adventure filled with love and powers that would make Superman jealous.

Here's the *"Formula:"*

1. Take one part of "Letting go" and add "give God everything"

2. Add the ability to see the real colors of this world

3. Mix in a solid plan of action to eliminate the negative and accentuate the positive. As you combine all these ingredients never give up, give out or give in.

4. Remove all your old baggage from the mix.

5. Stir in solutions while your eliminating problems.

6. Find a little mud to stir your daily problems into

7. Remember God's promise as the sun rises each morning

8. Imagine your world being full of opportunity

9. Plant only good seeds

10. Eat lots of brownies

11. Find others working on their relationship with God to fellowship with. And never give anyone your joy it's needed to make the formula work.

12. Be thankful

13. Give God anything that hurts you, so He can give you everything that heals you.

14. Mix this all together apply and watch the devil flee.

For the Son of God is come to save that which was lost

Matthew 18:11

Not come to save those who was lost, but to save "*That*" which was lost. What have you lost? He will help you find it again.

*Now unto Him that is able to do exceeding abundantly above all you ask or think, **according to the power that worketh in us***

Ephesians 3:20-21

According to the power that works in us. He can do exceeding abundantly above **ALL** we ask or think.

What's your greatest dream? He is able

What are you hoping for? He is able

What help do you need? He is able

There is nothing that you need or want that He cannot provide.

He is able

With man it may seem impossible but with God all things are possible.

But…remember… **Its according to the power that works in you.**

All God is asking is that you hand over the controls to Him. He can't take you where you need to be if you are constantly taking over the controls and steering the wrong way.

He not only understands spiritual warfare he dictates and dominates satan and all his traps. Things that are impossible to you are possible to Him. Nothing stands in His way. Except you.

YOUR 10ᵀᴴ SECRET MISSION

Your final mission is to Let Go and Let God help you to a brand-new sunrise. A place where your future will be unbelievable, and you'll be unstoppable.

Because were His children all He is asking is for you to come home and sit for a while. Your Father has it all worked out. You can do it I believe in you. You can *"**Become a Kid Again**"*

So, don't ever quit believing that miracles happen. You're worthy of His love. He's standing right in front of you with His arms wide open.

May God bless you on your journey and may you never quit dreaming, while you're finding new ways to the moon.

A Moment of Mirth

A businessman was in a lot of trouble. His business was failing. He had put everything he had into his business. It had become so bad that he even contemplated suicide.

As a last resort he went to visit his pastor and poured out his story of tears and woe. When he finished, the pastor said *"Here's what I want you to do. Get a beach chair and your bible and drive to a local beach. Take the chair and bible and set at the water's edge. Put the Bible in your lap. Open the Bible and let the wind rifle the pages.*

Once it does the Bible will come to rest on a page. Look down at the page and read the first thing you see. That will be your answer and will tell you what to do"

A year later the businessman went back to see the pastor and brought his wife and children with him. The man was in a new custom-tailored suit, his wife in a mink coat, his children shining. The businessman pulled out an envelope stuffed with money from his pocket and gave it to the pastor as a donation for his advice.

The pastor was curious.

"You did as I suggested?" he asked

"Absolutely" replied the businessman

"You sat in a beach chair with the Bible in your lap?"

"Absolutely."

"You let the pages rifle until they stopped?"

"For sure"

"So, what were the first words that you saw" said the pastor

"Chapter 11!"

You will find more happiness growing down than up.

Red Devine

The best remedy for those who are afraid, lonely or unhappy is to go outside, somewhere where they can be quiet, alone with the heavens, nature, and God. Because only then does one feel that all is as it should be. (from section nine April 27,1944 to August 1ˢᵗ, 1944)

Anne Frank

Sir, my concern is not whether God is on our side; my greatest concern is to be on God's side, for God is always right.

Abraham Lincoln

If God can work through me, he can work through anyone.

St. Francis of Assisi

Material possessions, winning scores, and great reputations are meaningless in the eyes of the Lord because He knows what we are and that is all that matters.

John Wooden

People resist change because they focus on what their giving up, instead of what they might gain.

Red Devine

God is a verb, not a noun.

R. Buckminster Fuller

I want to know how God created this world. I am not interested in this or that phenomenon, in the spectrum of this or that element. I want to know His thoughts. The rest are details.

Quoted by Einstein's former student Esther Salaman in "A talk with Einstein," Listener 54 (1955), 370-371 – Albert Einstein

I cannot think that we are useless, or God would not have created us. One God is looking down on us all. We are all children of one God. The sun, the darkness, the winds are all listening to what we have to say.

Geronimo

Things can go wrong at times. You can't always control your attitude, approach, and response. Your options are to complain are to look ahead and figure out how to make the situation better.

Coach Dungy

"Second star to the right and straight till morning."

J.M. Barrie-Peter Pan

The Price

T he costliest item you'll buy isn't a million-dollar home, a car that goes sixty miles per hour in 3.7 seconds, a jet, a boat, or even a private island. It'll cost you everything you have. It cost me my first marriage, my second business, and more than one broken heart.

I was looking for solutions to problems there were no answers for; lost, confused, wandering, wondering how I had gotten here.

Walking down back roads on cold winter days, lonely and silent, except for the sound of crushing snow under my feet, while a cold, bitter breeze passed by. Its constant presence pushed me forward as I walked three steps back.

I finally found a beach at 4 am; sitting there drinking cold coffee with no cream, feeling the darkness, seeking the light. As my half-eaten Egg McMuffin sat next to me catching cold from exposure, I covered myself with a blanket to stay warm. Sitting there uncomfortable, watching the ocean carry on its relentless bombardment of the shore, the sand desperately trying to hold on.

I sensed its struggle and felt its pain.

Then on the horizon the sun rose; its warmth encompassed me. As the dawn broke, hope arose with visions of wisdom and strength enlightening my senses. I'd just received the gift of another day. Love resurrected in my heart, I became enveloped in an uncommon peace, an undeniable faith. Rising to feel the sun, being warmed by its presence, I pondered the regret, the journey, and the lessons that I'd learned when traveling those broken roads. Leaving empty hearts behind.

As the light destroyed the darkness it was a revelation. There's something to be said about the quest, the unmitigated pain, the unforeseen challenges, and the improbable paths that led to this incredible moment. Sensing God's arms around me, realizing how profound life had become. I began to understand truth as wisdom. It emerged within my soul and comforted my spirit.

We're created to travel these roads, to seek the truth, to find distant memories and present dreams. Sometimes finding pain on roads that led to late night Nashville walking towards Memphis in the rain. Feeling nothing but blue.

I made turns where there were no roads, leading to the past I needed to forget and tried to remember. Hoping to find my way back home.

The shadows of seconds lived reminded me of what I was and what I had become. Drinking lattes, driving nowhere, texting my thoughts, trying not to feel swept away by the words, hearing but not listening. But now seeing the shadows in the light.

Life is a great adventure; traveling through hard nights and soft days leading to this morning full of joy, learning more when I cried than when I laughed.

Dreams die if we let them. Be brave, climb, and scale the highest mountains. Run to the highest peaks, no matter how difficult the path may seem. It's then that the view takes your breath away. As the sun rises warming your heart, lighting the way. In that moment reach out and touch the face of God.

There'll be blessings in the rain, healing through the pain; searching for words to pray. Sensing what's wrong or right, enlightened by the dawn's revealing light.

It's these times that give you the key to the map that leads to the road, that completes your quest as you rise from the dust.

Hungering for truth, searching under every stone, tearing down every wall, breaking every chain that bound you.

Understanding life is not about finding yourself but creating yourself. Learning to laugh, to cry, to care, never giving up, giving in or giving out; living life to its fullest. Finding the heart and soul of a child. Sensing the sunrise, full of promise and wonder; a place where frogs jump and kites fly; where you never stop asking why.

There are mountains to climb, and roads to travel, and since there are roads, there will be paths leading to a valley where you will find the answers you've been looking for.

Gaining the knowledge of who you were. Grasping the promise of who you want to be. Understanding the truth that He is God. It's then that you comprehend that the journey was worth it.

Standing as the sun sets in the west, fight to help others find these same roads, showing them the map that leads to the truth that changes tears into joy, fear into hope, and pain into peace. Helping them comprehend that God's love changes everything.

As you walk into the sunset you now know that it was the journey that mattered after all. The only dreams that come true are the ones you make true. You've found your way home, gaining simple-truth realizing how the river feels as it gets to the sea. And though the journey cost you everything, regret nothing.

Because you will be comforted by the fact that it was well worth the price paid.

Believing in miracles is the only path to receiving one.

Who we were, and who we are, and who we will be, are three different people.

Trust in the Lord with all thine heart and lean not unto thine own understanding. In all thy ways acknowledge him, and he shall direct thy paths

Proverbs 3:5-6

Our greatness lies not so much in being able to remake the world, as in being able to remake ourselves.

Gandhi

Kite Building Time!!

WHAT YOU'LL NEED:

- one 24-inch wooden dowel or lightweight, straight wooden stick
- one 20-inch wooden dowel or lightweight, straight wooden stick (hint: longer sticks can be cut to length with adult supervision)
- a large piece of paper (at least 26" X 26") or a heavy-duty trash bag
- tape
- lightweight string, twine, or fishing line
- craft knife (requires adult supervision!)
- ruler
- pencil, pen, or marker
- scissors
- ribbon

WHAT YOU'LL DO:

Step 1: With the craft knife, carve a notch into both ends of each wooden stick.

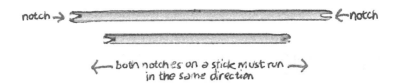

notch →   ←notch

← both notches on a stick must run →
in the same direction

Step 2: Take the longer wooden stick. Using a ruler mark off a spot that is 6 inches from the end (or 1/4 of the way into the stick).

6 inches

Step 3: Take the shorter wooden stick. Using a ruler mark off a spot that is 10 inches from the end (or halfway into the stick).

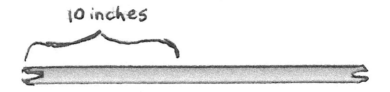

10 inches

Step 4: Place the shorter stick crosswise over the longer stick, matching up the marks you just made. When the sticks are laying down, all the notches should run parallel to the ground.

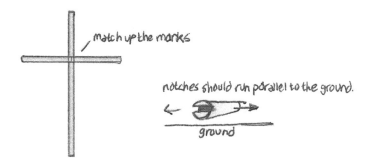

Step 5: Take the string and wrap it tightly around the center of your sticks, binding them together. You will be making an "X" shape with the string. Double check that the notches remain parallel to the ground.

Step 6: Thread the string through all the notches, creating a diamond shape. Wrap it around twice, making sure the string is taut. This is the frame of your kite.

Step 7: Pull the end of the string back towards the center of your kite. (Make sure the frame is still taut.) Wrap your string tightly around both sticks (mimicking the "X" shape you made earlier with the string) and tie it off with a knot.

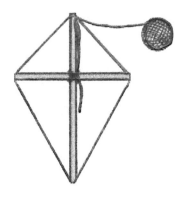

Step 8: Cut your paper or plastic bag so that it is slightly larger than the kite frames.

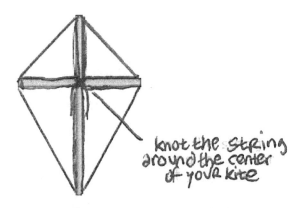

knot the string around the center of your kite

Step 9: Fold the paper over the string frame, and either tape or glue it down.

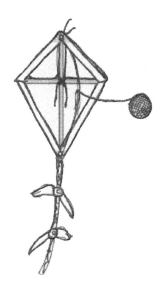

Step 10: Reinforce the top and bottom tips of your kite with tape. Then, using a pen or needle, punch a tiny hole through these reinforced tips.

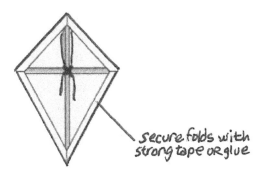

secure folds with strong tape or glue

Step 11: Cut a 2-foot piece of string. Knot one end of the string through the top hole and the other end through the bottom hole. This will form the bridle of your kite.

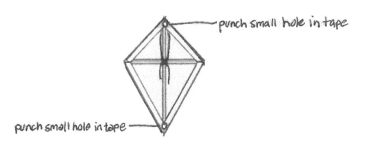

punch small hole in tape

punch small hole in tape

Step 12: Take the remainder of your string. Attach one end of it to the bridle (about 1/3 of the way down). This will be your flying string.

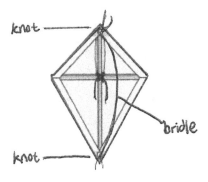

knot

knot

bridle

Step 13: Either tape or knot a 2-yard-long string to the bottom tip of your kite. Then, take your ribbon and tie bows around the string. The tail of your kite will add stability when it's in flight. Now, it's time to fly your kite! Let the wind work its magic!

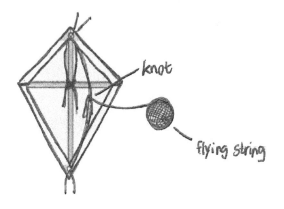

Answer to the Puzzle on page 220

R e s o l v e I t !!!- Resolve your problems don't show them off, don't brag about them, grab your problems by the throat and resolve them, create a plan and stick with it.

- *Quotes by Albert Einstein were used with permission from the Albert Einstein Archives, July 28th, 2015. Barbara Wolff, Information Officer, The Hebrew University of Jerusalem*
- *Quotes by Jean de la Bruyere are in public domain.*
- *Quotes by J.M. Barrie (Peter Pan) were entered the public domain in 2007. Refer to letter from The Great Ormond Street Hospital Children's Charity; London dated August 3rd, 2015*
- *Quotes by Ralph Waldo Anderson are in public domain*
- *Quotes by Napoleon Bonaparte are in public domain*
- *Quotes by Seneca are in the public domain.*
- *Quotes by Abraham Lincoln are in public domain*
- *Quotes by Francis of Assisi are in public domain*
- *Quotes from Anne Frank's Diaries were quoted from Section Nine April 27, 1944, to August 1st, 1944. Written permission to use quotes given by Barbara Eldridge of Anne Frank Fonds/ Geschaftsfuhrerin/Executive Secretary in letter dated August 12th, 2015*
- *Quotes by Geronimo are in public domain*
- *Quotes by Mark Twain are in public domain*
- *Quotes by Coach Dungy used with permission*
- *Crayola Crayons, Lucky Charms used by permission*
- *Quotes by Ruth Watson used by permission*

About the Author

Red Devine's family was not dysfunctional they were crazy. Raised in a hurricane wind, jostled about in a tornado until nothing made sense. Life was a challenge at an early age. But amid the storm was a feeling. A feeling that someone was watching over him.

It was a warzone, where no one was winning any battles. Dug in by alcoholism, abuse and his father cheating on more than his taxes. There was nothing Christian about his family except the Christian Brothers brandy his father drank.

Through it all there was a determination to be and do something different.

Then there was Linda. Linda was a stone-cold fox and sat in front of Red in his second period typing class. To this day he blames Linda for not knowing how to type. With fear and trepidation, he asked her out after class. She said sure if you go to church with me. This led to finding Christ and receiving Him as His Lord and King. He fell deeply in love with God and Linda became a lifelong friend. He found that someone.

Called to preach he worked the streets of Oakland through the Peniel mission at the age of fifteen. It was plain to see the devil's handiwork among drug dealers, prostitutes and the homeless. He attended Bethany Nazarene College and eventually preached throughout the south.

Great lives can be created by great difficulty it's the Genesis of learning the deepest secrets of the kingdom. His first marriage was destroyed through Bi-Polar Manic depression that his wife dealt with and he tried to cure. She eventually died at a young age from breast cancer even as they tried at times to bring the marriage back together. But God is good and through a series of events he met his soul mate his second wife and they have been married for over 20 years.

He is a writer, a radio host, an artist but above all deeply in love with God. He had left the "official" ministry to try and save his first marriage and began working in the corporate world. A top salesman, supervisor and eventually a director leading the Mid- Atlantic division for a major US corporation he was extremely successful. Eventually traveling the U.S. as a national sales trainer, writing and speaking new innovative ways to manage and sell.

Which eventually led to him owning his own successful business which blossomed until the crash of 2008.

Receiving the "National Businessman of the Year" awards two years in a row, nominated as a Kentucky Coronel invited to the White house with other business leaders for dinner with the president. He was mentioned in business management books at the time for his success in creating new ways to manage.

But the calling never left. Instead of speaking to hundreds at one time his ministry became speaking to one person at a hundred different places. It became a traveling ministry living in 20 different states working over 80 different jobs. At each location there was a need and by God's grace many times that need was met. Ministry is not always a suit, a tie and a Bible speaking from a pulpit. In fact, it is an everyday event in all our lives if we would just listen.

From raising a dog from the dead in Florida to healing broken hearts nationwide he traveled all fifty states, Puerto Rico, the Virgin Islands, Mexico and Canada. But God was not finished.

His main calling was to heal broken hearts, helping others find their way out of the darkness. To make the world aware of the devil's tricks and the evil that encompasses our planet.

He believes that every moment of life, every person he has met enriched his life with their stories. And he worked hard to enrich their lives with the life that Jesus led. Each life and every story along the way was another piece of the puzzle until all the pieces came together creating a beautiful picture. His calling and travels helped him find the answers he'd been searching for.

It's these stories that made him such a good story teller. But more than that he's found a place of peace and power that could only be accomplished by venturing out where broken lives and torn up families lived. Defeating the devil's intention helping those around him understand his tactics and ways. So, they can live an overcoming life based on God's love and the incredible freedom that comes from letting go and letting God.

He believes when we get to the pearly gates Peter is going to ask us to tell him a story if you have none to tell then you'll be in a quiet place in heaven. Will be there for eternity they'll need great story tellers. So he traveled many roads to find the secrets of the kingdom. And now God has called him to write and share the road traveled. Early on a word was spoken that in his later years God would renew the call and He has. Now as a writer and speaker sharing the challenges of life and the overwhelming power and love of God that always wins the battles and ultimately wins the war.

There is no greater power than God's love, no greater freedom than the redeemed heart, and no greater truth than His word.